Drowning Like Li Po in a River of Red Wine

Selected Poems 1970-2010

by A.D. Winans

Bottle of Smoke Press

Drowning Like Li Po in a River of Red Wine
Copyright © 2010/2017 by A.D. Winans

ISBN 0-9777300-9-3 (Paperback Edition)

Cover image is from a photograph by Aleksy Dayen.

Bottle of Smoke Press
Post Office Box 66
Wallkill, NY 12589
www.bospress.net

Table of Contents

A. D. Winans On A. D. Winans

I was born in San Francisco, and have lived here almost my entire life. I was born at home, premature. My mother said the doctor told her I would not live a long life. Now I'm 74 and the doctor is long dead.

My father was seventeen years older than my mother, and they fought constantly. When my mother wasn't yelling at my father, she was yelling at me. This left deep scars which is reflected in my book Scar Tissue.

My mother was born in Canada and was smuggled illegally into the U.S. when she was three years old. When she later tried to become a U.S. citizen, she was told by immigration officials there were no records of her entry into the country, and was advised not to pursue the matter or she might face deportation. She died a woman without a country.

My father had a difficult time expressing himself. It was my mother who took me for walks in the park and to the movies. My father didn't like his job as a gripman on the Municipal Railway and frequently called in sick. The fondest memories I have of my childhood were the times we gathered in the living room to listen to our favorite radio shows. (The Green Hornet and The Lone Ranger) and the occasional weekend trips to Alum Rock and the Russian River. However, the good times were few and far between, in what can only be described as a dysfunctional family.

I was a misfit in both grammar and high school. I was shy and largely kept to myself. I spent time at the public library, where I discovered the works of Jack London and daydreamed of shipping off to sea and writing of my own adventures.

I joined the Air Force in 1954 and was assigned to an Air Base Defense Unit, which doubled in peacetime as an Air Police Unit. I spent three years in Panama, where I saw the President of Panama assassinated and a dictatorship supported by the U.S.

There were three classes in Panama: The rich people who frequented the gambling casino at the Hilton Hotel; the middle class comprised mainly of Chinese immigrants who owned the shops and small restaurants, and the lower class who lived in squalor and poverty in the downtown area.

It was while serving in Panama that I became disillusioned with the American system. Panamanian canal workers, who performed the same work as their American counterparts, were paid less than half the going pay. In the American controlled Canal Zone, the U.S. Governor refused to allow the Panamanian flag to fly alongside the flag of the United States. Elections were rigged and ballot boxes were found floating in the canal.

The Joseph McCarthy era, the struggle for civil rights, the treatment of the American Indian, and the Vietnam War all became fodder for later rebellion, which resulted in the many scathing political poems I have written. I was honorably discharged from the military in February 1958, and returned home to discover the Beat generation.

I found a part-time job working at the post office and attended day classes at City College of San Francisco, graduating in 1962 from San Francisco State College (now University).

I began reading the works of Camus, Steinbeck, F.Scott Fitzgerald and Hemingway, and later became interested in poetry after discovering Ginsberg, Ferlinghetti, Corso and other Beat poets and writers.

While attending college, I spent my nights in North Beach, spending long hours at City Lights Bookstore browsing through underground magazines and books by established and emerging Beat poets and writers. I hung out at Mike's Pool Hall and drank at the Coffee Gallery and Gino and Carlo's Bar. My favorite hangout was The Place, where "blabbermouth" night was presided over by Jack Spicer, an evening event where poets and philosophers could get up and speak their minds on any topic that came to their head.

I met Richard Brautigan at Gino and Carlo's Bar and frequently saw Bob Kaufman at the "Co-existence Bagel Shop," where he held court. I frequented the Anxious Asp and was the first feature poet at the Coffee Gallery, receiving five dollars and all the beer I could drink. Discovering North Beach opened up a new way of life for me. It was the training ground for my becoming a poet and writer.

In the sixties and into the early seventies I worked at a variety of jobs, none of which were to my liking. The lone exception was when I received a coveted CETA (Comprehensive Employment and Training Act) position with the San Francisco Art Commission, Neighborhood Arts program, where I worked from 1975 to 1980.

In the seventies, I started up Second Coming Magazine and Press, which began in 1972 and ended in 1989. I served three terms on the Board of Directors of COSMEP (Committee of Small Magazine Editors and Publishers), which later became the International Organization of Independent Publishers.

These were exciting times, with annual conferences bringing together poets, writers, editors and publishers from all across the country. Thanks to my CETA position, I was able to organize poetry and music events throughout the city, including the 1980 Poets and Music Festival, a three county, seven-day festival honoring the late poet Josephine Miles and the late Blues musician, John Lee Hooker.

I met a lot of poet and musician friends and engaged in conversations that lasted into the early morning hours, but the truth is I find it difficult talking about myself. I prefer to let my poems do the talking for me. Too many poets perceive their craft as a "holy" mission, seeing themselves as prophets. That's a hard message to sell to the homeless and downtrodden souls that walk the streets of our inner cities, or the working-class men and women struggling to make ends meet.

My poetry largely addresses issues of concern to millions of Americans who spend the majority of their lives struggling to survive in a society bankrupt in spirit and moral fiber, where money is the only common denominator.

Early in my life I was influenced by the writings of T.S. Eliot and William Carlos Williams, but my mentors were the late Jack Micheline and Charles Bukowski, and to some extent, the Beat poet John Weiners, whose book the Hotel Wentley Poems (1958) moved me deeply.

I have never worn the label of poet well. It's not a word I'm comfortable with. It carries a connotation that somehow the poet walks on a higher ground than the average individual. Too many of today's poets are more concerned with publication credits than the human condition they write about. The truth is I would not be a poet if it were not for these strange voices camped inside my head; demon voices that confront me and demand that I write down their thoughts. The finished poem often bears little resemblance to whatever I initially had in mind.

The demons simply invade my thought process and take over. In this, I share Jack Spicer's philosophy that "verse does not originate from within the poet's expressive will as a spontaneous gesture unmediated by formal constraints, but is a foreign agent, a parasite that invades the poet's language and expresses what it wants to say."

I have been both blessed and cursed by the inner voices (demons) that possess me. I've never kept a notebook or used a tape recorder for future reference and I seldom write in long hand, although this may be in part due to my poor handwriting. Many people have called me a "street" poet. I suppose this is because much of my subject matter has dealt with life on the streets. I don't think this is an accurate label. I have been writing for over four decades and my style continues to evolve. The subject matter is as diverse as life itself. The form and technique I employ can and has changed from time to time. The one constant is that people remain my favorite subject matter. If John Weiners was a poet's poet, I'd like to be remembered as a poet of the people. My poems and my life are one and the same. They simply can't be separated.

Being a native San Francisco poet, I know the streets of this city like a gambler knows when to hold and when to fold. Jack Micheline wrote in a foreword for A Bastard Child With No Place To Go:

> "A. D. Winans is a man in search of his soul His compassion and love for his native city San Francisco shows in his poems. A. D. takes us on a journey of lost souls in the cruelty of a large city. He writes of the people he loves: poets, musicians, and the ordinary souls who have moved him. He knows the wars, the lost hookers, the crazies, the victims, and the ones gone mad. The system and the tragedy of America."

There it is in a nutshell. I'm not a guru. I don't go to the mountains looking for the Dalai Lama. I create largely in isolation. I write out of a sense of loneliness and sadness and anger, but also with love and humor, the latter for which I am indebted to the late Bob Kaufman.

I write with the same observational intensity as Charles Bukowski, yet entirely unlike him. Like Bukowski, you will never have to search in a dictionary to understand my poems.

I try in the most direct manner possible to say the things I have felt and experienced in life, and hope that the reader will find the voyage a memorable one. The noted writer Colin Wilson said:

> "Everything I read by A. D. Winans fills me with pleasure because of a beautiful natural and easy use of language—he seems to have an ability which should be common but which is in fact very rare to somehow allow his own pleasant personality to flow direct into the page."

I believe this statement to be true, but acknowledge too that my personality is not always a pleasant one. Sometimes the anger cuts through and severs an artery, but I believe this only serves to make the poem stronger. In essence, I write about life, its ups and downs, the laughter and the tears, the real and the imagined, the good and the evil in man. I don't pull any punches. I simply try to tell it the way it is, from the 9/11 tragedy to the homeless plight on the streets of America.

Poetry and writing have kept me going all these years. They have been the wife and children I've never had. I've had over fifty chapbooks and books of poetry and prose published and have appeared in over a thousand magazines and anthologies. I've given countless readings and made lifelong friends. None of this would have been possible if I had not discovered the magic of poetry. I believe in the long run my poems and prose will tell you most about who I am. As I said earlier there is no separating my poetry from my life.

I get up in the morning, have a cup of coffee and read the newspaper, spend a couple of hours at the computer, pick up the mail at the post office, take a half-hour walk, return home, listen to my jazz records, put in a few hours of writing, and then it's time to go to bed and get up in the morning and start all over again. That's what life is pretty much about. The growing up, the learning, the wild years, the mellowing, the settling into a routine, and then one day it's over. I'm satisfied with my life and the way I have lived. Writing poetry has helped keep lady death from my door. The demons are still there inside me, but I no longer let them control me.

I don't think any one man's life is really that important, but what he does with it and leaves behind is. I hope I have earned more good karma than bad karma points. I hope in the end I can look death in the face and say I've played the game honestly and that I never sold my integrity. In the end integrity is all a writer has. Sell your integrity and you've sold your soul to the devil.

Selected Poems by
A.D. Winans
1970-2010

Carmel Clowns
1970

CARMEL CLOWNS

Carmel clowns walk the street
Hippies try hard but can't look beat
Normal Norm plays Trick or Treat
While the Universe grows gargoyle feet

FLOWER DREAMS

In Golden Gate Park
In San Francisco
I leaned over
To pick a flower
And found myself
Staring in the face
Of a part-time policeman
Part-time gardener.

I tried to ignore him
Concentrated on the flower
Which was nearly as tall as I
And reached out toward the sky.

I leaned further on over
To sever its roots
Found myself attacked
From all sides
Lost one ear
One eye
My nose
Part of my scalp
And nearly all my sense.

I struck back bravely
Sought the aid of the gardener
Who smiled with evil intentions
As he handed me his shears
And leaned over to watch
Me take the flower's life.
I took the gardener's instead.

ODE TO GOD

God
is a
Sunday
Comic strip
Character
Little Abner
going down on
Daisy Mae
and tasting the
lipstick kisses
between her legs
and ordering one
just like her
for his son
who prefers
Carmel popcorn
served on
Jewish sesame buns
sold over the counter
in Argentina
by Nazi warlords
left over from
World War Two.

I HAVE LOITERED

I have loitered at city parks
watching old men pick their noses
in the twilight of their insanity.

I have observed old women
fumble in broken-down purses
for non-existent dreams.

I have watched young children
play in scarred sandboxes
destroying sand castles
like soldiers at war.

I have observed growing boys
slide down snake slides
chased by keystone cops
sniffing lethal gas
on death's window ledge.

I have Watched
    Listened
        Observed
Only to return home
And close the door.

LADY DEATH

Silly, fat old woman
Melting from decay
Sitting drunk at a table
Caressing a wine bottle
And wishing it were more
Dark, wrinkled skin
Deep, double chin
Breasts once were hard
Buttocks taut and firm
Gone, lost forever
In the darkness of night

BETRAYED

I saw you
Superman
Exposing yourself
In a Chinatown
Alleyway
On a sunny
April fool
Morning.
Dick Tracy
Didn't think it was so funny
He had you by the balls
Until you convinced him
You were working on the side
Of the law
And sent him down to Vesuvio's
To arrest a madman
For masturbating in the street
You should have told him
King Kong was down there
Taking a private leak
You should have told him
King Kong didn't like cops
God Damn Man
How can I ever hope
To believe in you again.

I REMEMBER STILL

I remember still how wonderful it was
Running to join each other's dreams
Sharing our separate worlds of hope
In rooms of music where angels lay

I remember your doll house dreams
Your lips colored with flowers
My hands tracing the valleys of heaven
And finding them within your silent
curves

It was a work of abstract art
A garden of unsurpassed beauty
I became God himself
And having you
I did not need a son

HIGH ON A HILL

High on a hill
In Diamond Heights
On a silly street
Named Laidley

I sit alone
In a dimly lit room
Adding to my thoughts
Of yesterday

Outside it is cold
I see the night fornicate
And commit cunnilingus
With the Universe

I sit in total darkness
The lights turned off
A normal person
Of normal I.Q.
Normal desires
Normal hunger
Debating the rage
That dwells within me

It is hard reading in the dark
It is hard trying to find things to say
I think I shall charge a dollar a head
For those who wish to visit me
There will be no charge for Jesus
Or young girls who wish to rub their breasts
Against my chest
Out of foolish curiosity

You who know what I mean
Can come and go
Untroubled through my dreams
There will be no charge for you.

Tales of Crazy John
1975

crazy john was a local poet of some repute
slightly paranoid with a laugh that never
failed to frighten the establishment and
their highly trained psychiatrists who
recommended he open a hotdog stand
in downtown san francisco but it turned
out he couldn't handle that either.

it seems he kept on serving meatless buns
sold to him by overweight nuns threw in
a little onions a stalk of celery or two
then stood back in wonder when the
angry crowd yelled:

You must be mad.

crazy john begged me to take him
to see his first baseball game until
i reluctantly agreed and purchased
two tickets to watch the dodgers and
giants knock heads at candlestick
park before a capacity crowd of over
fifty thousand

in the ninth inning with the score tied
at five and five, crazy john chanted
a magic incantation, and i know you'll
find this hard to believe, but so help
me god, jesus came down off a cloud
and stole home plate with the giants
winning six to five

things like that seem to happen when
you're around crazy john

crazy john liked to dance in
the rain
he liked the way it felt and
tasted and the weatherman being
somewhat unpredictable
he invented his own cloud
and sent it high into
the sky but the town people
were angry considered
it an intrusion on their normal
way of life

so crazy john gave in to
the insistence of
the town council and moved
it to the woods where
it rained almost continuously
and soon strange flowers began
to grow inch by inch moving
silently toward the city
where crazy john could be seen
dancing a raindance only
flowers understood

crazy john used to draw large crowds
at his yosemite camp sight after word
got out he ate a breakfast consisting
of two cactus plants, a lizard, a bald
headed eagle and a prairie dog over easy

after washing it down with good old mountain
dew, he would smile at the masses, belch
out loud, sing god bless America and disappear
down the mountain riding bareback on a grizzly
bear scrawling graffiti on the nearby redwood trees

crazy john gave in to the unemployment offices
insistent demands and took a job as a conductor
on the skunk train in not so far off mendocino
where he spent the better part of the day chasing
frightened passengers down the aisle trying
to punch holes in their hands and gather tongues
for baggage checks

they kicked him off in reno where he lost his
fortune at keno and found himself in the black
mountains of dakota panning for fool's gold and
selling used road maps to german stuka pilots
looking for lost dreams

they say crazy john is
mad because he claims
to converse with
the ancients grabs
strange girls off
the street and tries
to sell them his peripheral vision

sometimes on a warm
summer night people
come from far off
to watch him gather
fruits and nuts at
the local farmer's
market

but its been many years
since i've seen him
perform a miracle

he claims he's waiting
for the holy ghost
to come out
of hiding

they locked crazy john up
in a padded cell where three
doctors took notes
with unbelieving eyes watching
him create butterflies
from building blocks
then turn into a frog
forced to devour his creation
in order to survive
in the morning when
he changed back again
he had three doctors
for company

Straws of Sanity
1975

FOR KENNETH PATCHEN

where were they when you lay in your deathbed
crippled and dying
where were they when you lay starving and broke?

there was no wailing then
there were no sounds of wild lament
not even a quiet weeping of the soul

no hungry hands knocking at your door
as you lay looking up at the heavens
barely able to talk or move

where were they when the hour of darkness came
when the blackbird sang out in disguise
and the bullfrog in the field silently cried

strange how the vultures gather here like blind ravens
crawling the lonely streets with their midnight cawing
gathering in twos and threes to read their swollen lines
here at north beach where the written word dies slowly

no real sign of emotion in this bought and paid for audience
each poet following the other like a line of corpses strung
out ten miles in a neon lit graveyard each voice rising and
falling the coated sugar on their tongues intent on mourning
down the hours on this moonless midnight evening where terror
and agony are partners and the shadow of your being dances
along the mountains coated in bright enamel.

FOR CHARLES OLCOTT

He'd been a computer engineer
and a good one to judge his resume
but he'd been unemployed for months
and he'd been despondent too

And yesterday they found the body
of Charles James Olcott Jr thirty-
five beneath an oak tree a plastic
bag over his head and his resume
job applications and rejections
nearby

Olcott, Father of three children
formerly owned his own business and
before that worked for R.C.A.
Crocker Citizens Bank
Varian Associates and other firms
in the field of data systems and
programming

The search for employment was
discovered in papers scattered nearby
and in a small briefcase at his side

A graduate of San Francisco State College
with a major in languages and extension courses
in computer engineering at the University of California

Just last week the President gave a talk on the
state of the nation and assured the folks at the
commons club that 5% unemployment was healthy
for the economy

Charles James Olcott Jr was not among those
seen applauding

THE LAST COWBOY

they say he's just another oakie
out of place in the city like
hank williams would have been
in reno, nevada

he's traded in his horse for
a run down car, no six guns
at his side, just a used guitar
and a worn black leather case

the smell of beer and saturday
night brawls has replaced the
cowshit that once covered the
trail that now leads only
to another endless bar

just another oakie they say
or perhaps the last cowboy
left in america

you can find him any night of
the week with a beer can in his
hand strumming his guitar for
fifteen bucks and all you can
drink

his face hasn't lost its smile
he still holds dreams in that
silver throat that sings out
songs to greet the early morning
light over the hardened streets
shaped like sandbags around
the soul

WINTER REFLECTIONS

tuned in the television set down the hall
and turned on the cinderella ball
wall street ticker-tape parade for moon men
broadway go-go girls doing the swim
burned children crying in my ear
vice president playing on my fears
facts and figures and more government lies
another commercial and another young boy dies
heroism found in vietnam fields
hospital costs rising according to blue shield
flowers grow and bloom
funeral horses strangle on gargoyle plumes
baby crying in the background
head so fucked up can't make a sound
latest love lays naked in upstairs bed
only one God Damn thing
going on inside her head

UNTITLED

I have sat too many evenings
watching
old men eat their last meal
one eye on the dessert the other
on the obituary column

STRANGE HAPPENINGS

Avant Garde says we like your style very
much it reminds us of Vonnegut and he's
no slouch but it's not what the boss is
looking for and Mc Calls says read your
work with great enthusiasm but we no
longer accept unsolicited manuscripts
We wish you nevertheless the best of
luck in placing it somewhere else and
then there is the Chicago Tribune who
says stunning sorry not for us not to
mention all the rest who say enjoyed
reading your work very much sorry
we can't use it.

But the funniest one of them all is from
the friendly local press who says nothing
and sends me back some another poet's work

All the Graffiti
on All the Bathroom Walls
of the World
Can't Hide These Scars
1977

BADLAND WOMAN
(for anne)

she's there bringing bad memories
like a carnival sideshow freak
she brings you back to
the worst days of your childhood
like a parent intent on making
you pay a long-overdue debt

her eyes are a pair
of vacant suitcases waiting
to take you nowhere

the songs she sings
belong to a forgotten
hollywood matinee idol

she walks your dreams breathing
heavier than an obscene phone caller
carrying her wounds around
like a harpooned sailor

a bandage stuck to rotting
flesh

40TH BIRTHDAY

i seem to remember wantling writing
a poem about how
he never wanted to be a poet that
he would carry a lunchbox just
like the rest of them if only
the strange mutterings would leave
him alone

now at forty
i feel pretty much the same standing
naked as a deadman's shadow wishing
i had been blessed with
the skills of a union carpenter instead
of these heavy words locked away inside
these aging brain cells

forty years old feeling
like the worn impression on
a buffalo head nickel holding on
to these fading visions
like an immigrant unable to escape
the old country
the moods coming and going
like cloud banks sinking slowly
like the "titanic"
the ghosts dancing on the deck dressed
in words of fire

and as each day brings yet another illusion
harsh as a hobo's dreams
i sing the song of my chosen grave
the lines dancing

like a ballerina on
a high tension wire

while a friend of mine considered
a success in the business world
tells me that like him
i should make a list of priorities
and stick by them no matter what
but the hooks are too far in
too high up into the gut
to do anything about

a poet is like a train
a romantic trip back into another time
he is good for a laugh or two
someone to converse with/occasionally
sleep with/and always someone to stay
away from/when he is down and out

america is no place for
a poet to grow old in
a poet is not a thing
i would want my child to
be

D.A. LEVY WAS DEAD RIGHT

it's all a lie nothing
changes
the trees shed their leaves
like a summer t.v. special
the undertaker goes about
his business
the walls hide messages
like greedy beggars
the doorbell rings
nothing changes
it is all the same

the old man is thinking of death
the young man is thinking of riches
poets have become exotic merchants
of death

butterflies are beautiful
they have no desire to fly
to the moon
like kaufman says
poets don't sneak into zoos
and talk to tigers anymore
it is perfectly all right
to cast the first stone
if you have more than
the other person

the avon lady walks on water
the blind man sniffing
his way up her leg
nothing changes

the boxing matches
the bullfights
the football games go on
and we go on too
like a tired tongue resting
between the legs
of a very bored
woman

the truth of the matter is that
d.a. levy was
right
                "some people
just cannot beat the system
                and poets
can't even pretend they are
beating the system"

I PAID $3.00 TO SEE BUKOWSKI READ

I paid $3.00 to see Bukowski read
then went around to the side exit
and got in free
sat behind stage on an old piano watching
the old man sit at the table drinking beer
and facing his enemies
his hero worshipers reading
one good poem for every three
bad ones and
the audience not knowing
the good from the bad
and after it was over after
his admirers had cornered him
for his autograph and whatever else
they could get out of him which
was nothing

he smiled took my arm
and said,
A.D.
i want to see you at the party
and then climbed into the van with
the young kids who envied him
the young poets who said
his poetry was the shits
the young kids who hated his guts
the young kids who told him how
great he was
the young kids who wanted to
be seen with him
and one or two who wanted
him dead

and so i refused a ride in
the van not feeling comfortable
with undertakers who drive
live corpses to sealed graves
before their time
and got in my own car instead
and drove up across van ness
across the streets of
my home town
and arrived at the party
a half hour late
and "buk" was getting blown in
the bathroom by a pretty middle-
class hostess who probably gargled
listerine

and it was wall to wall bodies
and the usual crowd
the young poets who were jealous
of the old man
the young poets who seek instant fame
the young poets who would never make it
and the young women who had made it already
once too often in bedrooms and hallways
in alleyway and in johns with pushed
up skirts and knees scarred from
one too many head jobs

and the old enemies were there too
john bryan edging his way across
the room whispering low key
"you better watch it my wife is here
carrying a knife"
and hank shrugging it off

and saying that was in
the old days in
los angeles
can't you forget?

and of course
he couldn't because
hank had made it and
he hadn't

and the poets from berkeley
and the poets from los angeles
and the poets from san francisco
and max schwartz
the only man trying to get into prison
when everyone else is trying to get out
and the homosexuals
and the groupies
and the leather clad crowd too
which included one chick with
her shriveled tits hanging out
and her male slave wearing
a dog collar

and then i grew tired
and started to leave
when i was introduced
to this rich girl from australia
who travels on her father's money
and lives on castro street with
the homosexuals and fucks those
who aren't

and she's got a pair of tits
that stand out
and she opens her shirt and shows
them to me and says that
she can't drink alcohol that
she's on antibiotics
and coughs and sneezes
and i figure that
she has a cold
and then she's clutching me
and shoving her tongue down
my throat
and i'm dry humping her against
the wall
and she has her hand on
my cock
and I have my hand down
her blouse
and she has a half-foot
of hardness threatening
to roll a lucky
seven

and she pulls back
licks her lips
smiles and says

i shouldn't be wasting your time
you remember the antibiotics
and I nod my head
and she says

i've got the clap
it won't be cleared up

for several days
but I liked your poem

the crazy john postcard
i had given her and
i nodded my head

do you have a phone number
she said
and i nodded yes
and she took it down
and said:

i'll call you when
i'm well
and left the room
to french kiss this
dude in the hallway
who maybe
she wasn't going
to tell

and so I went home alone
and beat off on the bed thinking
of this girl from houston that
i had a good thing with
a week earlier
the one buk had paid
$300 to fly to
san francisco because
he thought
he was in love with her
and she thinks
she is in love with me

and me being too tired
to be in love with
anyone

the loneliness of
the clock ticking down
the hours
like an old organ grinder playing
the final chords at an unattended
funeral

NORTH BEACH POEMS
1977

FOR PADDY O'SULLIVAN

Paddy O'Sullivan
home again wearing
the scars of the past
like an engraved bracelet
passed on from one lover to another
walking the streets of north beach
in search of old visions now only
memories in the nightmare mirror
of madness—swapping tales
with obscene priests hung over in
the drunkenness of eternal failure.

Paddy O'Sullivan of Kerouac tales
and Cassady visions
Paddy O'Sullivan walking
Washington Square
the bulldozer death lurking everywhere.

Paddy O'Sullivan does your typewriter
still talk to you in
the lonely hours of the night?

Paddy O'Sullivan alone in
San Francisco
city of suicides past and present
waiting for that lady poet
who will forgive you in the morning
for forgetting her name in
the hour of dawn when our needs are soothed
with the power of the written word
that stirs moves inside us
like a runaway express train stalled

on the freeway
like the haunting breath
of a hound dog closing in for
the kill.

Paddy O'Sullivan where
have all the poets gone walking
straightjackets trapped by time
the sun is not as you see it now
everything changes and yet remains the same
the streets are no more or less intense
the lines on your face are the lines
on my face as we move back into
the body into the inner flesh measured by
the amnesia of yesterday.

this town coughs up its dead most rudely
the raw nerves of time returning to haunt me
oblivious to the thirst lying still at
the edge of the river.

the blueprint of our life etched in
the dark shadows of
the soul.

FOR BOB KAUFMAN

Room full of poets, writers, philosophers
drinking the hours away at Spec's bar here
in north beach this cold weekend night
Vicki and the great felony artist waiting
for Fairfax Alix and the midnight party
Patchen's old lady and books translated
into a hundred tongues

A table full of beatnik memories
old testament prophets
Micheline and yes you Bob Kaufman
come out of the evening shadows
out from beneath your safe withdrawal
that makes you walk these streets no
longer filled with wonder

sitting at the table reciting yeats
and eliot micheline calls you a titlist
but more than one poets ego is like the
resurrection here at Spec's with the table
running over like the last supper but there
is no rooster to crow your betrayal black
jesus of the fifties

sitting here blinking yesterdays nightmares
a tear came to my eye drinking tonic water
instead of rye calculated madness in the air
no place to dance rainbows buried in the alley
the old gods mixed in with the new

Your long years of silence broken
a prisoner of war come home to tell all

a prisoner of war walking the streets
of north beach
a not so pale ghost come home to tell it all
tell it all eliot and the tea room ball
your dreams of america are dead
they killed them slower than any war
your dreams of america are deader than
the electricity they shot through your head
in hospital rooms where the blood ran black
not red
but tonight you are alive
thin and trembling like a pale ghost
the protruding veins of your skull
working out their poetic skill
eyes dilated lips trembling
giant come home to taunt
the soldiers
here at Spec's
new but not so new words from the head
soft angel eyes carrying the burden
of past murders on shoulders stooped from
the executioner's sword

FOR VICKKI

sweet lady
of north beach
body slender as
a picket fence

come crack my skin with
the tenderness
of your tongue

let my fingers be
the warmth between
your legs

you dream of smoke
i'll dream of fire

in the morning
when your defenses
are down

i'll promise
not to hurt
you

CITY BLUES

in the back room they sit talking
laughing a poet with a broken
arm nursing a tired grin in
the shadow of an even more tired
afternoon

phantom faces mocking the hours
away in a country that kills
its poets and whose poets kill
each other

a city of sober comedians whose
children resemble w.c. fields
in a city where laughter is
everything and poets a dime
a dozen

FOR JILL

walking naked into
the bathroom after
an hour of love making

you tell me that
i'm the best lover
you've ever had

one foot raised to
the sink
like a panama whore

the washcloth wiping away
the seeds
of lust that disappear
faster than
the seconds on
a clock

later
the itch returns
as we adjust our bodies to
the height
of acrobatic limits

the flesh trembling
like two tightrope walkers
strung out on
speed

NORTH BEACH POEM

out into
the harsh night into
the lonely streets
of north beach stoned
on words walking
the streets of san francisco watching
the old people make their way to mass

old men and women leaving behind their sins
dressed in simple hats and death black shawls
bowing to the holy eternal mumble
of dead saints dressed in gold thirsting
for the wine that is denied them

the ceiling a giant mirror hidden in
the skulls of expressionless monks laying
in glass coffins
hands folded in ecstasy
eyes open smiling like a stoned gypsy
hanging from a pendulum in
the chapel of hope where italian priests
weaned on dago red ply evil thoughts from
sterile minds toying with
the heads of the masses staring always
staring searching for paradise
fat and content smoking tijuana slims
stone faced magicians on their way to
the graveyard where semen ejaculating
altar boys mock the hunchback crawling
on scarred knees three steps behind
the screaming organ grinder with
the one-eyed monkey on his back

san francisco
home of my birth where
iowa scarecrows peek through broken
windows at overheated stallions breathing
hard down the necks of sweating dwarfs lurking in
the back yard of grace cathedral where
the hangman's shadow stalks
the altar boy with neon signs of insecurity

no dogs allowed
no parking between nine and five
keep off the grass
do not enter
out of order
one way
do not disturb

ford smiling
kissinger smiling
justice bound and gagged in Chicago

youth cult found inside pants pocket
of man claiming to be
ponce de leon

walking the night
walt whitman in search
of sherwood anderson lost
in clown alley sniffing used
ashtrays

whore screws
cocksuckers delight
ten dollars a night

hank williams twenty years
ahead of his time

robin hood strung out on speed
breastless majorette with greased
thighs caresses phallic baton stuck
between plastic legs

fat ass politicians selling
their version of freedom
bent over with the weight
of their medals

up, up and away

superman is alive and well
at gino and carlo's disguised
as a dissipated italian gone
mad on kryptonite

here on grant and green where
the black and white hustle nightly
a cargo of restless souls for
city prisons late midnight
special

chinatown lamps
oriental intrigue
do chinese women really
have slanted cunts?

the tong won't tell you
they're too damn busy
selling lottery tickets

down in shanty town

the left
the right
the overground
the underground
all busy ripping off
the other while
the penis fantasy
of a vaginal orgasm finds
clitoral satisfaction in
the extracted womb
of the madonna hung
out on the clothesline
to dry

2 a.m.
young men standing half out
of their heads
young girls in jeans and
see-through minds

old men not all that old stare
vacantly at the moon at
the women who carry their souls
in their eyes

walking past central police station recalling
the holding cell where young "ed"
i never knew his last name picked
at his head cracked open by
a barker in a broadway tunnel
of love

walking to crazy john's place sharing
a glass of wine sharing even
the paranoia chatting with
frank at the bus stop on
my way back to mission street
his eyes as large as
the owl who haunts
my dreams'

you can find them all here
on any given night
an all night orgy
no invite needed

crazy eugene who crushed
the skulls of those who
disagreed with him but
who went to oregon and
found himself in
the eyes of his children

peter with dreams
of picasso who walks
the open artery
of a dying wound

lorraine stoned on
coke and meth
alix back from petaluma
to recite
mc beth

here in north beach where
they took eddie away and

gave him three years and
eyes that weep blood then
set him free again
one thousand-ninety-five
days and nights
of cell and sodomy with
only a handful
of angry poems that
no longer crack
the looking glass

here in north beach where
they come and go suffocating on
the water of sound

home of paddy o'sullivan
forgotten legend
of his time

home of bob kaufman giant
of a north beach that
no longer exists

home of Jerome whose visions
of nexus faded in
mendocino state hospital where
you can't always tell
the difference between
a smile and a scream

home of ben although
no more who after ninety
days treatment
they drove thoroughly mad

no doubt for his own good
when they traded him straight up
his heritage for
a feather bed

but it need not be here
it can happen anywhere
like they ran in
jack micheline for
pissing on a cop's foot
in new york city
for biting a law man's nose
but they couldn't kill
the poetry and prose and
now he's back twice as dangerous
as before

and they messed with bukowski's face
for offering them salvation and grace
not understanding anything but guns and mace

but they can't take away the soul of vickki
of pale thighs and eyes that know no lies
vickki whose good times i have shared and
whose pain i have known
nor the spirit of the woman of one-eighty-five
whose deeds are legendary

and yet they took away inez
who few if any of you recall

inez of fine breasts and limbs
of fire who died alone in
a beatnik san gottardo hotel hall

they took away d.a. levy's life pulled
the trigger as sure as his own because
he was human enough to believe
he could change this land

and they took the life
of ed lipman but could not break
his spirit for
he knew the secret of invisibility something
the hound dogs can only smell

from broadway to mission street where
the pigs are a different breed junkies
sitting at the doggie diner needles
in search of sunken veins making their
own dreams their own buddha their own
jesus christ

to them city prison is just another room
where the cockroaches crawl sideways up
the wall on their way to
a beggar's coffin where
the bones are many

working my way home from north beach
to upper mission passing
kell's place where
the lonely man of music lies arms
tight around his woman's head
to keep the clouds of death away
so that at least she might sleep

home at last
safe from the self-appointed gods

of my destiny tired
of what they want for you and
me when it is really them

tired that they will follow me to
the grave their sons of death bringing
more death to mine

at a time like this
it is good to be alone
no one to camouflage your feelings
bandage my dreams

hung up on my own disappointments
like an animal playing solitaire
with his shadow

the hi-fi playing low and kind deadening
the screams of my mind oblivious to
the outside ferris wheel revolving around
the universe housing fragile bodies moving
like silent boxcars across angry railroad tracks
where lonely souls drag themselves along
the freeway scrambling like wounded animals wrapped
in fear and angry poets spit out funeral wreaths
at scarred clouds passing slowly across
the face of the moon

ORG - 1
1977

POEMS OF PASSION COME HARDER EACH YEAR

stoned in Austin on grass and good vibes
the passion passes through my skin
like raindrops searching a wishing well
while down at the conference hall
paperweight publishers and poets
dance through another day
with ideas as sterile as surgical gauze

THE FURTHER ADVENTURES OF CRAZY JOHN
1980

released from the nut house
crazy john took the courts advice
stopped off at the state department
of rehabilitation and signed up for
a course in fingerprint identification
walking the streets for clues insisting
he was the direct descendent of
sherlock holmes that
the answer to life lay hidden in
the crematory.

the cops not buying it and remembering
him from an old mug shot hauled him before
the magistrate who sent him back to
the home for the criminally insane where
he took refuge in the piano playing
old caruso songs reciting Bukowski by
day and mc kuen by night.

the old folks dancing in the halls
the echo reaching the ad-min office
who ordered him removed taken back
to court where he was given
a one-way ticket to reno nevada.

all but the crippled street hobo
avoiding the look in his eyes.

they found crazy john a job telling
fortunes at a san mateo county
gypsy parlor
the first time they crossed
his palm with silver
he got up and left

"wait,"
the elderly woman complained
"where are you going?"

to seek my fortune he smiled
disappearing into
the crystal ball reappearing
five years later in
a lifeboat salvaged from
the titanic

crazy john showed up in russia
one leap year dressed as a frog
popping valium and blaming
the croaking of frogs for
his lack of sleep

jumped in the deep end of
the swimming pool reappeared in
the children's end bobbing
for apples before returning to
eureka california to take
the job of state game warden
vowing to reappear every
four years secretly plotting
the taking of
the mad czar's dreams.

crazy john was found waltzing alone
in the long abandoned avalon ballroom
warned to leave by the night watchman
he joined him in the fox trot
the two step
the ali shuffle
the old rope-a-dope itself
his eyes two candles lighting
up the night

in the morning they found the guard
lying exhausted on the floor
crazy john smiling still dancing
around the room accompanied by
the music of long forgotten orchestras
playing delicately in the wings

crazy john was excommunicated from
the church for preaching that
jesus christ was really
cecil b. de mille
thrown out of congress for claiming
that abe lincoln was really john
wilkes booth in disguise
forced to leave in disgrace
he left for australia in search
of a mate who might bear him a son
who would perpetuate
the impossible

THE REAGAN PSALMS
1984

reagan appears on
the capitol steps
his mind wanders back to
hollywood
u.s.a.
his eyes blink like a pinball machine
his lips move in puppet-like precision

the white house staff passes by
they are dressed in crisp uniforms
goose-stepping along with
flags in hand

nancy reagan appears on the balcony
she is dressed in high heels
and is made up to look like
shirley temple as
she waves to the cheering
courtesans engaged in serious
conversation with the pope

below in the courtyard
a man is seen hanging from
a rope
the flesh of politics stapled to
his lips

reagan turns enters
his chambers turns on
the t.v.
there is a riot in the streets
but everyone looks like
charlie chaplin
the odor of death seeps through

the antenna as the
reagans retire to bed
in the morning
they wake
drink a glass of sake
switch back on the
t.v. and are greeted by
a string of corpses walking backwards into
the walls
led by a midget carrying
the flag of Hiroshima in
his eyes

El Salvador and
Nicaragua waiting in the
wings

POLITICS

going to be a reagan stamp
one of these days
old man tells me at
gino and carlo's bar
in between my second and
third drinks

you can't beat these damn
politicians
he says
but reagan will be
patient
he's going to be a stamp
one of these days
perforated holes in-
between
the spaces on each
sheet

guess that's
the only way to
lick the
son-of-a-
bitch

THIS LAND IS NOT MY LAND
1996

LACKLAND AIR FORCE BASE

at Lackland Air Force Base
in San Antonio Texas
the DI told us that the
Korean War was not over
the truce notwithstanding
said that the commie hordes
had no code of honor
and could not be trusted
to keep their word
so they separated some of us
myself included
and assigned us to the elite
Air Base Defense School
taught by ex-marines
one kid was weaker than the
rest of us
worse yet he was a pacifist
they took him out on the rifle range
stripped him down to his shorts
and had him shoot at moving targets
for hours in the rain
a week later he came down
with pneumonia
spent three weeks in the base hospital
and was later dropped from the school
the military intelligence boys
questioned us for days
but no one betrayed the
code of honor
for we were trained to obey
and honor was second only
to the kill

PANAMA FOUR

Panama City could have been
Any slum city in America
Run by corrupt police and politicians
But when you add the American troops
Sent there to safeguard the people
It was worse than any slum
You might imagine
Shacks for homes
Naked children playing in the street
Twelve–year old boys selling pictures
Of naked women being fucked by dogs
Or selling their ten-year old sisters
Taxi drivers taking you to the fabled
Donkey show
Or to the homes of young whores
While less than ten miles away
In the American Canal Zone
It's hometown U.S.A.
The Governor's Ball
U.S. civilian police
White skinned women sipping coffee
And tea
Armed forces TV selling the
American Dream

AFTER THOUGHTS

1955...
The President of Panama
gunned down at the racetrack
for building schools and roads
and thinking of the people
U.S. troops from nearby bases
issued guns and sent to town
to assist the Panamanian
National Guard

two-hours into forced insanity
I sneak off to the Amigo Bar
smoke a joint in silence
try to shut out the madness
until I become oblivious to what
is happening outside
half the army looking for an assassin
the other half too stoned to care

the sweet smell of Mary Jane floats
through the air, fills the bar
as I put the safety on
and lay my rifle to one side
smile at the bargirl
on the other side of the bar
not knowing whether she would
like to make love to me
or put a bullet in my head

RETURNING HOME FROM PANAMA

they had this bar at Ocean Beach
called the Chalet
it used to be a hangout for Vets
the American Legion boys
mostly fat and balding
middle aged
one so old he claimed
he was gassed in WW 1

you never knew whether to believe
him or not
he just sat there staring talking
into his beer
humming that song:
"Over here Over there"
and using terms like doughboy
and pill box
and you just somehow knew
he had been there
was still there would always
be there

AMERICA

drummed out of the infantry of death
I came back to you carrying
the poems of my soul
opened the door of life
and found only death inside

America
I have read the State of the Union
and listened to the state
of the economy
in a state of hysteria

America where the
poor and the black are sentenced
to Attica and the rich serve time
at San Clemente

America where the coal miner's lungs
are used for corporate profit
where the only sound that can be heard
is the opening and closing of the downtown
Bank of America

America where the angry voices
of suburban mothers can be heard
preparing their children for death
amidst the hurried jerks of masturbation
from the closets of the university

America where blank faces move
like a pendulum in a grandfather's clock
pointing in the direction of the once

proud hobo now standing in line
in hope of becoming an S.P. Detective
riding free the slick super chief special
out of San Jose.

America where the elderly are treated
like railway boxcars
kept idle unemployed
forced to walk the streets
like an unacceptable poem.

America
it is hard living in a country
where the hours are shaped like coffins
the law and order administration running
wild in Waco Texas

America where the politicians
sold the country to I-T and T
and left the people with buffalo
stew and scientology
Reader's Digest has renewed
its option on the education system
the mafia weans the poor on drugs
while IBM and Coca Cola
are busy competing for the nations heart
as cancer and cardiac arrest
ride high on the charts followed closely
by DOW Chemical and DDT
a hard combination to beat

America where the
Narcs of New York City spawned
from a generation of gangsters

grow fat on the fears
of countless junkies

America where holiness is found
in the bowels of Buddha where
Christ died on the cross
and the police were quick
to take his place

America
I listened to your
Bi-centennial message dripping
blood like a butcher's apron
heard the drums salute the
ghost of Custer calling
her children to muster
the magic OM of Ginsberg
buried in the bowels of capitalism
that doesn't know the difference between
a poem and a dollar
the American way
if you can't kill them
buy them into the system

America
I grow older carrying
a new found vision
invisible to the human eye
the years grow heavy
in the cavity of my heart
left feeling like an army mule
hauling a cargo of death
each new year sweetened with
my own blood

America
you are the only country
I have known
for any length of time
and unlike others
I have no desire for Russia
Cuba or Prague
But I am a man
I am a poet
I am the energy running through
your withered veins
all too aware of the
storm troopers of justice
who would turn off the beauty
like a rusted faucet
these men in blue who
sniff the blood of my wounds
like a hound dog crossing
a river of blood
their sirens playing sad tunes
outside my window
like a poet forced to read underwater
until twice dead and once resurrected
the poet turns over in his grave
but the middle finger he raises
is jammed back down his throat
until the shit he shits is theirs
and the blood they bleed is his
and the cries united fill the air
like a lonely bird lost in flight

THE CHARLES BUKOWSKI /
SECOND COMING YEARS
1996

POEM FOR THE OLD MAN

I tried to picture him
battling leukemia
but still managing just
20 days before his death
to send a poem
to Wormwood Review
filled with life
to the end
perhaps a wry smile
on his face
for the doctor
and a hand on the ass
of the nurse
playing out the game
to the end
like only the old man
was capable of doing

LOVE COMES IN MANY DIFFERENT FLAVORS
1997

The whip master is waiting
It's time to atone for your sins
Get down on your knees
And beg repentance

Refreshments will be served
At the conclusion of the
Black and Blue Ball
Swim suits are optional
Shackles a must
Crosses in the shape
Of Christmas trees
Will be made available
For those with hammers and nails

Leather clad porters will be there
To punch your ticket.

The climax of the evening
Will coincide with
The orgy master's late arrival

S AND M GAMES THREE

It began when
he was in Catholic school
And his cock got hard
When the nuns rapped his knuckles
With a ruler
For infractions of any kind
Harder still at boy's military school
Where the head master
Had him drop his pants
For the stinging paddle
On his bare ass

It took two decades for him
To find the right mistress
Who understood his needs
Serving her every desire
Dreaming of castration
His balls bronzed and worn
Around her neck
But for now he settles
For the ball-buster devise
And a turn on the rack
Hot wax flowing down from
His cock and balls
Visions of those nuns floating through
The purple haze of his childhood

VENUS IN PISCES
1997

MAKING IT WITH MY BABY

Let the wagging tongues wag
And the loose lipped zombies
Say what they will
We'll sing to each other
In the still of night
While calico cats stoned
On poems
Run through our dreams
And rainbow drenched clouds
Drag themselves across
The sheets with
The falling away of our clothes

FOR LADY LYNNE

Lennox days and nights
Lodged in my skull like
Tiny splinters beneath
A hang-nail

My mind stoned
Feeling like Merlin
The Magician on
A starless night

Hair falling over shoulders
Lost in a whirlwind of desire
That comes and goes like
A mad man's dreams

My words empty
As a tramp's pockets
As you allow me
To walk the lining
Of your soul

Making it one last time
To the music of a thousand
Crickets rubbing their hind
Legs in applause

UN TITLED

On the beach near Mendocino
I watch you wade in to the ocean
Skimpy wet bikini clinging
To your curves revealing
A trace of pubic hair
That stirs my passion
Makes me think of how
We were to be married
Even now wanting you more
Than life itself
Not as a possession
But as a permanent fixture
Till death do us part

At the age of 60 that
Still seems possible
You only 32 afraid
Of those two words
I DO.

You say that things will change
That it won't be the same
Sex a tasty pizza will become
A dog's bone
Soon the sun will set
And I will cover you
With a blanket
Slip inside you
On top or from behind
Try once again
To shut out the doubts
That leaves my head alone
With poems that cry out
To touch you

ON BREAKING UP WITH SHEILA

9 hours a day at work
Another hour counting down
The hours
Commuting to and from work
Dodging angry motorists
With middle fingers
For brains
And when I unlock the door
And sink down on the sofa
And listen to the angelic voice
Of Billie Holiday
My mind tells me
That I need a drink
Maybe many drinks
Various ghosts chewing on me

Later I tell myself
I'll haul my tired ass over
To the typewriter
Sip on a glass of white wine
Try to pen a line or two
Trying to put off going to bed
Forever forced to remember
Your smell on the sheets
The taste of your flesh
Your warm back on mine
So I hit the typing keys
Trying with words
To still the pain
Of what I need
And never had
My mind my need

My weakness
No different than
Any other man
Thinking of love
Thinking of fucking
Thinking of you
Pounding out my regrets
On the typewriter
Savoring the lush taste
Of creativity
Hot as your flesh
Feeling the weight
Of your memory
Heavy as an anchor
Tied to the tip
Of my tongue.

SAN FRANCISCO STREETS
1997

LOOKING BACK

When I was young and down
And out
And wrote of pain and agony
From first hand experience
From a studio apartment
On the fringe of lost souls
Hookers dopers and low life
I was told by people of affluence
Who enjoyed hanging around writers
That this was good for me
That great writing came from this
And that someday I would look back
On those days with fondness

At the age of fifty-nine
I've moved up to
A one-room apartment
In a hip neighborhood
With photographs of Josephine Baker
Billie Holiday
Martin Luther King, Junior
And the Kennedy brothers
Adorning the walls
To remind me of my life
Time commitment
To civil rights

I've managed to stash away
A few bucks in the bank
And my icebox and closets
Are full
And at one point

I was knocking on the
Door of success
A door that never quite
Fully opened.

Now when I think back
On those days
It's not with any sense
Of fondness
Though I can't deny
That the women
The drugs and the parties
Were fun
And the words rolled off
The typewriter
In magical splendor
But the people of affluence
Drifted away too
The apartment and the
Lack of money
The roaches and the mice
Were more circumstances
Than necessity
And they didn't bring creativity

You can go forward
Or you can go backward
But the smell of shit
Is still the smell of shit

Art creates itself and
I don't think I'll ever look back
On those days with fondness anymore
Than a stockbroker welcoming
The 1929 stock market crash

SOUTH OF MARKET

You can see
From the look in his eyes
The scar on his face
That he's someone
You don't want to mess with
His eyes survey the scene
Like a periscope
He's a two-bit thug
Looking for action
An old time beat cop
Looking for a head to bash
He's Boston Blackie
And Al Capone rolled
Into one
His women are mean and lean
Bred on the S & M scene
With tattooed flesh
And black mesh
They walk the seedy side
Of town
Looking to do the last
Waltz with you
In a back alley
At South of Market street
Or in a basement dungeon
It's all the same
All part of the game
Doing a tap dance
On your spine
Looking dead serious
Like a sumo wrestler
Sizing you up for
The kill

GOING BACK IN TIME

I was looking at my scrapbook
The other night
While listening to an old
Woody Guthrie record
Scratchy as a smoker's cough
After twenty years of lung destruction
And there I was in my youth
Hitchhiking from California to Arizona
And places further West
Heading in so many directions
That it was like getting lost
In the trick mirrors at the fun house

And there were the women
Then young girls
Free flowing spirits
Who gave their minds and bodies
At the slightest invitation
And nights too laying alone
In tangled sleep
Feeling like a deer caught
In barbed wire
Or sitting bunched-up
Cold and disheveled
At the local Greyhound station
Fighting off the eyes
Of leering men who preferred
Boys to women

Now sixty
I realize I was there and back
So fast

Like a derailed train
Running out of track
Returning home
Carrying my life
In a knapsack
The days the months
The years hung out to dry
Like your mother's washing
On an old clothesline

SAN FRANCISCO STREETS

I've walked these San Francisco streets
Like a cop walks his beat
My eyes taking in her every movement
My brain storing real and imagined changes
In sixty years her changes have not eluded me
She is older now
More wrinkled and cranky
Much like me
But the two of us manage to get along
Like business partners looking after
Each others interest
Market Street once a fashionable socialite
Now a gaudy whore
Mission Street once the home of the Irish
Now glossed over
Tough looking youths with dagger stares
Where you guard your wallet
Like a eunuch guards the harem door

You have to learn to give and take
You have to learn to adjust
The city is like a cup of strong coffee
Stir her enough
And the flavor floats to the top
I have walked these streets
All my life
In good condition
And broken down physique
Knowing there is no city
Like her in the world
She is like a pair
Of empty shoes

Sitting under the bed
With no feet big enough
To fill them
She is like a squirrel
Running between the live
Wires of a utility pole
She is like the last bullet
In the executioner's gun
She is like a room full
Of poets crazed with their
Own conversation
She is like Billie Holiday
Drenched in sweat
She is like the face of god
All forgiving
In her insatiable lust
For life

GIRLS OF THE TENDERLOIN

The girls of the Tenderloin
Wear tank tops and short
Tight skirts with white
Shoes showing off black skin
Or black shoes contrasting
Their white skin

The girls of the Tenderloin
Strut their stuff
From noon to three
In the morning
Sometimes later if the
Traffic allows

The girls of the Tenderloin
Stand out like a dragon in
A Chinese New Year parade
Moving their hips like
The hoola hoops of yesteryear
Talking heavy thick slang
Their "Hey baby
You want a date?"
Cutting through the air
Like a machete
Looking for a snake
In knee-high grass

The girls of the Tenderloin
Walk talk strut their stuff
Not afraid of the
Law man's bluff

The girls of the Tenderloin
Stop traffic
With their looks
Their dark brown eyes
Thirsty as a Mexican matador
Looking for a kill

THINKING ABOUT THEN AND NOW

when I worked in Modesto
back in 1964
I'd drive to Stockton
and sit in the park
drinking with the winos
in Salinas it was field workers
in Crow's Landing it was with
unemployed Mexicans at Latin
cantina's
in North Beach and the Mission
I hung out with deadbeats and
losers
street people fighting
cirrhosis of the liver
junkie tremors and now
AIDS
in the Fillmore
I cut my teeth on jazz
let Billie Holiday patch up
my bleeding heart
in the Potrero
I saw the last of the
factory workers
growing thinner
like their paychecks
fearing for their jobs
in the Tenderloin
I drank with whores and
prostitutes
who opened their pocketbooks
as freely as their legs
on Market Street

I witnessed panhandlers
crouched like criminals
in open doorways
a short distance from
the Jesus freaks with
billboards on their backs
pointing the way to heaven
at the old southern pacific
railway yard
I saw the last brake man
smoking a cigarette
eyes vacant as an empty
satchel
while on the other side
of town
high on top of
Nob Hill
society ladies sat in
chauffeured limousines
white poodle dogs nestled
between their piano legs
unaware of the dredges
of humanity walking third
and howard street
drinking cheap port from
brown paper bags
starving cold disheveled
as the homeless are today
waiting for god or pneumonia
to walk them to the grave

CALL TO POETS
1997

poets unite;
forget about a career
in poetry
and concentrate on the poem;
quit turning out factory assembly line poems;
quit trying to out-Bukowski
Bukowski.

poets unite;
listen to your brothers
and sisters;
quit being the first
poets to read and the
first to leave;

quit using words
as a preaching tool
when all over the world
people are starving dying
and committing genocide
as we stand on stage
well fed begging for applause
playing to the audience
telling our most intimate secrets
pretending to be knowledgeable
when we know so little;

rams out fucking sheep
poets playing trick-or-treat
politicians beating their meat
whores making it under the sheets
predators lined-up with elbow grease
landlords waiting to cancel your lease.
it's gotten so bad

you can't tell the real from the elite
Everyone has become a carbon copy
of themselves.

take a number
step up on stage
rattle the cage
let loose your rage
be sure to wear your page
the call you miss may be from
God
as we rival Ringling Brothers
standing tall
standing proud working the crowd
like carne hustlers.

I call for all poets
to put down their poems
for a year;
take a vow of silence
help an old woman across
the street
serve a holiday meal
at Saint Anthony's
quit sending out manuscripts
for six months a year
spend the saved postage
helping the homeless

sell your signed copies
of Bukowski and Ginsberg
and give the proceeds
to war victims in Iraq
pay homage at Malcolm

X's grave
ride a boxcar for
Woody Guthrie
say 12 Hail Mary's for Ali
sing a song for Selena
say a prayer for Burroughs
take the Eskimo out of Eskimo Pie
rename "hooters" bar
"testicles" and hire
male waiters to serve
in jockey shorts
legalize prostitution
campaign to have cops arrested
for disturbing the "peace"
tell the pope that
you're giving up drugs
and the church to worship
at the altar of Walt Whitman
make Patchen required reading
visit an animal shelter
save a pet from extinction
volunteer for meals on wheels
deliver food to the disabled
and dying
give up center stage
ego driven mania
for a trip to the park
at dusk

refuse to pay your taxes
invest in yourself instead
of interest bearing bank accounts
meditate instead of masturbate
make love instead of fuck

drop a bomb on Naropa
set fire to the poetry flash
to prove you're more than
a poet junkie

take a bookstore owner
to dinner
talk child talk
translate gibberish
put ego aside
put power aside
quit visiting Kerouac's
and Bukowski's graves
return to the world
of the living
put the poet back into
poetry
make me want to believe
in you again

REMEMBERING JACK MICHELINE
1998

POEM FOR THE POETRY POLITICIANS

hey Jack
the Poetry Flash finally
gave you some space
even if you had to die for it
they used your name in the same
sentence as genius
funny, when you were alive
you never heard that

the Poetry Flash
the Iowa Review
the Paris Review
the American Poetry Review
this is not poetry
what ever happened to
Whitman's wild children?

the Holy Grail has gone
the way of grand slams
con games and cheap scams
these people dance
with the dead
they have never had
a cup of thick black coffee
at an all night truck stop diner
or walked with holes
in their shoes
or sang the blues

they shop at Macy's
browse the Internet
they don't make love

they fuck
they don't eat food
they nibble
they don't drink
they sip
it's become nothing more
than an ego trip

you won't find them
in the Mission
in the Tenderloin
or South of Market
or standing in line
at the race track

they drink bottled water
eat sushi
trade favors like
baseball cards
they're living proof
of mediocrity in the arts

they're the gravediggers
of the Beats
playing trick-or-treat
they never miss getting
quoted in an obituary
they're the paparazzi
of the poetry world
always looking for
a photo opportunity

they don't know the
meaning of shame

to them poetry
is a monopoly game
hungry for money
hungry for power
hungry for fame
these would be mountain men
who set their traps with the skill
of a grave digger

this is the new breed
poetry politician
seasoned alley cats
hiding in sandboxes
sharpening their claws
looking for a back
to scratch
staking out their territory
like a vampire in need
of a fresh fix of blood

their faces are puffy
their handshakes weak
they hover in the shadows
like an undertaker waiting
to dress the dead
beware my friends
don't die
they'll be sniffing
at your grave

LOOKING FOR AN ANSWER
1998

BECOMING LIKE A BOXER IN MY OLD AGE

Tossing and turning in bed
Unable to sleep and when I do
The night sweats and dreams
Tear at my soul

Approaching 60
With an arthritic neck
My moustache turning gray
And the women turning the other way

Each year the poems come harder
Like a lifer marking time
My body dodging life's blows
Feeling like a boxer being asked
To take a dive
Being beaten up on knocked down
KO'ed
Each time getting up
Beating the 10 count
Knowing you can't win
Can't beat the odds
But refusing to throw in the towel
Nose bleeding head pounding
Jabbing punching going the
Full 15 rounds
Hoping to get something better
Than a draw.

POEM FOR THE POET WAITING ON FAME

Don't get up in the morning
Pissed-off bent out of shape
Defeated and fatigued
Don't kick your dog
A can is okay
Don't look for trouble
A fist in the face
Won't change history
Don't spit into the wind
It might come back at you
Never place your hand
Over your heart
The marksman might think
You're marking his target
Don't fight the poem
The typewriter is never wrong
Accept the inevitable
And maybe it won't come
Until next week
Next month next year
Maybe never

Remember there isn't anything
Wrong with being a mechanic
A cab driver a pimp
A whore

Be glad you have two hands
Two feet two eyes
Two ears
One of the latter is okay
If you name is Van Gogh

Go easy go slow
Or life will pass you by
Like an aging conductor
Without a train
Leaving you feeling
Like a comic without applause

Know this above all else
Seven out of ten poets
Are bores
And two of the other three
Literary whores

Support that odd one
He/she needs you
And you need him
More than either of you
Will ever know

TOUGH GUY POETS

You know who they are
They appear in the same magazines
Like hired bounty hunters
From the old frontier
No one is spared from their
Angry words which serve
As bullets for the mind

They fill the little magazines
Like sardines crammed into
A fat man's mouth
They talk about eating pussy
As if it were a vitamin supplement
Though their women might snicker
Behind their back

They do a lot of fucking with
The typewriter keys which usually
Translates into a lot of shucking
Oh they look tough enough when
You meet them face to face
Strutting their stuff
At cowboy bars
Half-way into a drunk
But when they sober up
They're little more
Than failed cowboys
Who were never invited
To the shootout
At the ok corral

FROM PUSSY TO POLITICS
1999

IN LEAGUE WITH THE DEAD

i pledged allegiance
to God
and all he stood for
i offered the pope
my first born
a free tarot reading
and 10% of future royalties

God countered with
a night on the town with
Mary
a contract with
Doubleday
and all the angel food cake
i could eat

BARBIE'S SAFE SEX COUSIN

She comes with instructions
plug into AC/DC outlet
mount when fully inflated
adjust speed to preference
at the height of passion
hold her legs back with
her soles pointing at the ceiling
for best results assume
a sit-up position
drive in like a piston
push the voice box mechanism
to hear her scream
the warm fluid she emits
will tell you she has cum
pull out slowly
turn her upside down
slap buttocks soundly
clean up spill with
moist cloth, deflate
put back in box
store in dry place
until ready to use again

KEN'S SAFE SEX COUSIN

Comes with easy
To follow instructions
No assembly needed
Follow easy instructions
Plug into AC/DC outlet
Pump attached bulb until
Desired size is reached
Sit, lay or straddle
Adjust control knobs
To desired intensity
When approaching climax
Push button under scrotum
Milk like liquid will expel
From penis slit
When satisfied deflate
Wash with soap and warm water
Pat dry
Deflate penis
Put back in box
Store in closet
Or under bed until
Need arises

LOYALTY

I will not pledge allegiance
to the flag of the U.S.
and everything it does not
stand for
I will not bow down
to corporate america
and its religious right
I will not/can not accept
your moral bankruptcy
your greenback god
buying and selling lives
on the stock market exchange
I will not bow down
to a country where assassins
determine the course of history
whose papal church
has its own bank
where ka-ching ka-ching
has become the new holy mantra

J. Edgar Hoover died in order
to get to heaven
and tap the private phone
line of god
secretly videotaping
jesus' every move

america
you are one big
insane asylum
your manic depressive
innkeepers waging war

on the masses
your henchmen standing proud
on your purple majestic mountains
kissing the cold stone faces
on Mt. Rushmore
looking like a mafia don
with the cold kiss of death
on his breath

REFLECTIONS ON BUKOWSKI

they come to pay their respects
lay flowers at the grave
some bring whiskey
or picnic there
engrossed in imaginary conversation
they say neeli wept and clawed
at the grave
his grief so great

no skid row memories here
the grounds well kept

they come alone
or in pairs and groups
a holy pilgrimage
on an unholy mission
hoping the messiah
might rise
and take them
in his arms

UNTITLED

The preacher man
don't believe in evolution
the conman
don't believe in revolution

The priest has run out
of absolution

No more autographs
No more forced laughs
No more hanging around the zoo
swapping stories with gurus

Going to smoke me some dope
with my good friend the pope

Going to make love nice and slow
read me some Edgar Allen Poe
lose myself in the late night show

Going to make a cameo appearance
on the 6 p.m. news
play me some John Lee Hooker blues

Going to penetrate a prerogative
bugger the cosmos
evolve evolution into a revolution

Put anarchy on the stock market
nuke technology
outlaw e-mail
declare Da Da the official
English language

Going to hang religion from a tree
make John Brown the
new national anthem
Turn outlaws into inlaws
Landowners into donors
put Bukowski's face
on Mount Rushmore
pay homage to a whore

Going to name a park
After Rosa Parks
put a little nookie
in every fortune cookie

Expose Saint Nick as a chick
with a dick
going to invite the First Lady
to ride through the streets of Chinatown
dressed in a see through night gown

Going to talk to the fly
in the soup
alone or in a group

Going to sing a ballad
with Lorca and a band of gypsies
stop off at the manager
and have a talk with
the Lone Ranger

Going to put an end to hemorrhoids
outlaw humanoids

Going to offer a truce
bring back Lenny Bruce
make politicians ride the caboose
going to go back to school
erase the golden rule
going to feed a vulture
starve off mass culture
going to turn evolution
into a revolution
make poetry
an institution

I KISS THE FEET OF ANGELS

dark starry night
fog creeping in
over the hills
raindrops falling
on the window
I see the faces
of old friends staring at me
ghosts from the past
freight trains steam ships
subway trains carrying
their cargo of dead
Rimbaud the mad hatter
Baudelaire
Lorca fed a dinner of bullets
Kaufman black messiah
walking bourbon street
eating a golden sardine
Micheline drinking with Kerouac
at the old cedar tavern
Jesus wiping the perspiration
from his forehead
the foghorn plays a symphony
inside my head
I hear the drums
I feel the beat
I kiss the feet of angels

BILLIE

Billie's a poet
but drives a cab
to pay the rent
driving men across
the border
to get laid
at Mexican whore houses
$35, the basic rate
for twenty minutes
with the house mom
banging on the door
to let you know
when your time is up

$150 to $200
for an all nighter
with Billie getting
a third of the take
depending on the
cantina

the Mexicans have a name
for what Billie does
"gancho"
which as close as I can tell
lies somewhere between cabbie
and pimp
no one ever said
being a poet was easy

WRITTEN ON THE BOMBING OF YUGOSLAVIA

it's history repeating itself
all over
from Napoleon to Attila the Hun
gothic nightmares
slaughterhouse mentality
old glory versus fascism
genocide versus annihilation
war criminals posing as heads
of state
masturbating messiahs
wearing the masks of Hiroshima
and auschwitz
the bones of women and children
fuel for Hitler's ovens
played out once more in kosovo
while corporate america stands
guard at fort knox

WATCHING MILES DAVIS PLAY
AT THE BLACK HAWK 1962

long wailing notes
that run up and down
the spine
makes you shudder
like a woman coming down
from a climax
heightens the senses
sends shock waves
through my body

God, Jesus and the
Holy Ghost rolled
into one

AFTER MY POETRY READING

this guy comes up to me
after my reading
tells me he's been reading
my work for decades
"You've written maybe ten poems
that stand out," he says.
"Ten poems out of a thousand.
What's that 1%?
You wouldn't make a bat boy
in the majors," he says.

Poor fool doesn't know
I write for the "little's"
Tonight I'll write number eleven
Maybe move up to Triple "A."

IT SERVES YOU RIGHT TO SUFFER
1997

FOR DINO

The Beach is dead
The blood thin red
Dino the bartender lives
In a graveyard
Chief undertaker
Dispensing pain
Like low grade cocaine

There was a time when
I might have invited him outside
Only the tough guy image
Long ago died

The Beach is dead
The poets have left
Dino the bartender
Walks with spade and shovel
Having found his niche in life

The Beach is dead
The ghosts cry in despair
Mad cowboys rope my visions
Hog tie my poems

The curse of Kerouac serenades
The demons of sleep
The Beach is dead.

GROWING UP IN AMERICA

As a child
I thrilled
To the railroad trains
Riding out of the badlands
Not knowing they were owned
By robber barons

I watched the calvary
Charge the indian villages
Like Attila the Hun
Believing Custer a hero
And Sitting Bull a savage

Not taught in school
About the deadly smallpox plague
Blankets traded Indians
For title to their land
The deadly plan to murder
An entire nation

Generations of ripped-off cultures
Gather in the museum of history
Dolphins die in tuna fishermen's nets
While pelican eggs refuse to hatch
Victim of man's greed and waste
As the blistered hands of faceless
Migrant workers reach out for recognition
Only to find death in pesticide laced food
The tools of revolution
Laid aside
Rusting from affluence
And false security

The dreams of a thousand
Proud warriors lay buried
In unmarked graves
No historical monument
Will make mention of them
Their children buried
In graves so small
Their parents wear them
In their hearts
Like an anchor weighed
To the tip of their tongues

FOR KELL

Old guitar slung around
His back
Pure country
Singing the blues
In all of us
With eyes that cry out
To be listened to
Nearly 66
Hard as the highway
By the same name
Leaving a message
On Annie's answering machine
Reading a poem about
A bird that died
In his hands
Remembering the scattering
Of his daughter's ashes
Caught in the pit of sorrow
This man of music
This one time old friend
Still fighting
Still scrapping
Like the rest of us
For whatever time
Is left

ON THE ANNIVERSARY OF THE DEATH
OF THE POET BOB KAUFMAN

The hollow sockets that once
Housed your eyes
Invade my thoughts tonight
As burned out images
Of the skull play
My nerve ends
Like a skilled violinist

How is it out there
Among the stars?
Are poets issued wings?

I had a dream that
I saw you driving across
The face of the moon
Picking up astral speed
As you reached a moon crater
Where God stood chatting
With Jesus

He had a cold beer
In his hand
And was resting next
To a lamp post
Looking like Bogart
Back from a night
On the town

Just before I woke up
I thought I saw you
Parachuting toward earth
Jesus riding your coat-
Tails

161

IT SERVES YOU RIGHT TO SUFFER

visions of the past
floating like dead wood
through the river bank
of my head
pink panties and
white bra
lying on the floor
next to the bed
drinking tequila
with glasses dipped
in salt
as I slowly moved down
your soft underbelly
like a moth undressing
a light bulb
feeling like a blind man
learning braille for
the first time
and I was there the night
you put your fist through
the window
swearing you saw god
in your own reflection
yelling mantras no one understood
as the people below the window
looked up and wondered
what the screaming was all about
I was there that night
at the bar when you hit the guy
by the jukebox over the head
with a beer bottle
leaving seconds before the cops came

and though I should have
I didn't give them your name

I was there the night at the graveyard
when you visited the grave of the only
man you ever loved
and as always you left a bad taste
in my mouth
like a blow job artist bent over
in a back alley
spitting out the seed
like an altar boy
hiding a wafer under
his tongue hoping
the priest won't catch him
in a lie

I was there the night
you sat alone
at the airport
with only twenty-five cents
in your pocket
watching people greet
their loved ones at
the arrival gate

I was there the night
they took you away
to langley porter psychiatric
clinic
where you soared like a bird
in flight
never to return
to earth as we know it

I was there the day the crucifix
carrying priest
said the black magic mumbo jumbo
words over your grave
looking like a caterer
serving food
at an unattended banquet

I was there the day
they buried you
in a shawl of unwritten poems
and I drank a toast to you
long after the others left
remembering that white bra
and red lace panties
the night we lifted boulders
from the chest of Jesus
and threw them in the face
of God

SCAR TISSUE
1999

UNTITLED

My mother rode the ferry
from Canada to the U.S.A.
at the tender age of three
Born of common English stock
A marriage arranged like
a mail order bride

Sex was for rearing children
Orgasm a 4-letter word.

Dad died in 64 the funeral
wreathe lying heavy
at my door
Mother left alone with
Homemade pies and dreams
turned to lies
Hijacked for a ransom
she could never pay

WAITING

The last few months were the worst
As if she were under a gypsy curse
Her children near and far
Forced to watch life flee her
Like a runaway car
Seeing her nibble
At each meal
Robbed of all zeal
One eye on the dessert
The other on
The obituary column

TRYING TO LET GO

A week after Saint Patrick's Day
You passed away
Yet remained in our hearts
Half smile
Half frown
Hanging around

I still visit your grave
On Christmas
Your birthday
And Mother's Day
Tied to death's umbilical cord
That refuses to let me go
Knotting itself like a noose
Around my neck
Too tight for comfort
Not loose enough
To set me free

REFLECTIONS

It wasn't until after my mother died
That I learned
She had been abused as a child
Which helps explain why she slept
With her clothes on
All those long years

The memories linger on inside me
The fighting that knew no end
My parents like Joe Louis and Max Baer
Until I grew up avoiding
All relationships

It wasn't until I turned fifty
That I realized
I was holding a loaded gun
To the head of every woman
I might have loved
Silently squeezing off live rounds
Of an angry childhood

The seeds I left behind
In those vaginas
Were bullets meant
For my mother's womb

POEM FOR MY FATHER

It took me decades after his death
Before I could write a poem about him
It was as if a small part of him
Had entered my heart
And remained behind the barbed-
Wire fence he so carefully constructed
Over those long years
Stayed there all that time
Building an invisible umbilical cord
Reaching out for un unseen love connection
Sending signals carried on the sealed lips
Of blackbirds circling invisible graveyards
Finding in death
What we had never known in life
Those ghostly white hands scratching upward
From the grave
Desperately trying to cup the tiny flame
Flickering inside the valve of my heart

FOLK HEROES AND OTHER
STRANGE HAPPENINGS
1999

THE LONE RANGER

The Lone Ranger
Was kicked out of the
Local chapter of the
A.A.
Drank himself into
A coma before
He was forty
Took to sitting around the
House a lot sipping wine
Watching Howard Cosell
Eye Alex Karras on
Monday Night Football

Was voted Halloween drag queen
Of 76
Married Tonto's sister

Was found murdered in
Chinatown by a deranged
Half-breed

DICK TRACY

Dick Tracy is walking down
Castro street in
San Francisco looking
For a good time

He has just come from
A night with Wonder Woman
And does not know
He is in homosexual heaven

A cowboy dressed as a cowgirl
Picks up Dick Tracy and takes
Him to his/her home

In the morning when
Dick Tracy wakes up
He isn't sure which side
Of the law he's on

LITTLE ABNER

Little Abner sits around the
Old Ozark wood stove
At the country feed store
His head filled with visions
Of the past
Talks with Joe Palooka
Wears a wide-rimmed straw hat
Hates Al Capp for dying
And making him a has-been
Watches his weight religiously
Reads the Washington Post
Looking for a message
From the holy ghost
Has sand kicked in his face
At every beach in the land
Lays Daisy Mae once a week
On Tuesdays in between reruns
Of Gilligan's Island
Likes sleeping alone
Remains a loyal yankee fan
A graduate of the class of
42
He waits eagerly
For the next class reunion
While down on Castro Street
In San Francisco
They whisper that
He can't get it up anymore
But when Dagwood's out of town
Blondie still comes around
Leaving him thinking that
He's the hottest thing in town

POPEYE THE SAILOR MAN

Popeye the sailor man
Liked to hang around the docks
After a full days work
Telling old sea tales
To young boys from the local
Merchant Marine Academy
Like the time he sold Olive Oil
To the Greeks during
The great depression
When Vaseline was hard
To come by

Had this fondness for fondling
His cock a lot
And unnatural designs
On this dude named
Wimpy
Who hung around
The hamburger palace

Rumor is that he took turns
With the boys gang-banging
Olive Oil on weekend nights
Died from a bad dose
Of clap revealing in
His will that
He hated spinach
All those years

Rumor has it this news
Was responsible for the
Stock market crash
Of 1929

REMEMBERING BUKOWSKI
1999

HEY BUK I GO TO THE RACES TOO

Got hooked on the racetrack
After reading your poems
Even though deep down
I know it's a sucker's game
It costs $20 just for admission
A program
A hot dog and a beer or two
And betting on a winner
Is like betting on the
Hunchback of Notre Dame
To make it with Madonna
The odds are about the same
But I have to admit
There's something about the touts
The vendors and the guy behind
The mutual window
Who looks a lot like
A Vegas gagster
That draws you into the game
And the horses
Those magnificent nags
Even the ones with blinkers
Offer us that long shot
Possibility of going
Home a winner
Standing near
The $2 or $5 window
Waiting for the
Warning buzzer
To plank down your bet and
For that one brief moment
That it takes to run the race

We become as one
The horse the jockey
And the betting man
And woman
Racing for the finish line
The winner's circle
The glue factory
Man and beast as one

FOR THE POET DOWN SOUTH

There's this poet down South
Who wrote this poem about
This poet up North
Who supposedly keeps attacking him
This poet down South learned
Of these alleged attacks from
A supposedly poet friend
Whose job it must be
To keep this poet down South
Informed of this vicious
Poet up North
Who keeps putting him down
And of course the poet down South
Doesn't question the source
But feels slighted enough
To put this poet up North down
Which isn't exactly new
For the poet down South
Old habits being hard
To break

This poet down South
Has an interesting theory
That he got lucky and made it
While the poet up North
Remained unlucky
And that this somehow
Explains the reason
For the poet up North
Attacking him

The theory of the poet
Down South is that you're
Better off with strangers
Who will allow you your luck
Be it good or bad
And that you should be careful
With whom you drink with unless
Your fate is to stay unlucky

The truth is that I know
This poet up North
He doesn't seem such
A bad fellow

For eighteen years
He published hundreds of poets
Including the poet down South
But I'm not surprised at the
Poet down Souths rantings
For as long as I have known him
It has been this way
If not against the poet up North
Then with poets East and West

The truth is that most of
The people the poet down South
Puts down deserve it
More or less
But it's equally true that
This poet down South
For the better part of his life
Has been a drunk
And for that matter
This holds true for the poet

Up North too
One became a respected poet
And the other a respected editor
Who writes poetry too
Though as the poet down South said
Never achieved fame

And having been a drunk myself
I can tell you first hand
That most drunks are not nice people
Not the poet down South
And not the poet up North
And never for one moment
Did I think that hanging around
With the poet up South
Was a cool thing to do
For the only thing worse
Than a bad drunk
Are two bad drunks
Which is why I only drank
With him three times
In nearly two decades
For to have palled around with him
Would have meant being harangued
Nevertheless I loved this man
And loved his writing even more
And that's all that really matters
In the end

And the poet down South
Did better than most men
I know
He wrote about his life
In a mean lean and honest way

But he wasn't the only poet
In the world
And one might think
He would have shown at least
As much respect as he demanded
From those he called his friends
And the poets who emulate
His life style
Must be lonely souls
For there's nothing romantic
About being a down and out
Writer
People who believe otherwise
Are only fooling themselves

What this poet down South represented
Was the American dream of making it
Rising out of the slums
And being able to spit in the face
Of the beast
Even if sometimes
The beast is ourselves

What the poet down South represented
Is individualism at its best
And at its worst
A crying appeal
To a popular audience
Who can empathize with this
Look man they can say
The poet down South made it
Maybe there's hope for me too
So you see
It isn't about being lucky

At all
The important thing is
That much of his writing
Shows empathy for the
Down and out
The damned and near
Damned
And not yet death trodden
Souls of America
For the drunks and
The working class stiffs
For the assembly line zombies
Barely able to make it home
From work at night
And this is where
The poet down South's art
Rose high above
The man himself
For his art was better
Than he was as a person
Which is a compliment
And not a put down
And only goes to show
That the power of art
Prevails in the end
And that my friend
Is what poetry
Is all about

PEOPLE YOU THINK YOU KNOW
1999

NIPPLES AND CLITS
(for Jennifer)

nipples and clits
nipples and clits
nothing satisfies my taste
like nipples and clits
have no appetite for cars
and ships
rather have a tipple
of nipples and clits
off with her shirt
up with her skirt
we'll play Billie Holiday's
top hits
while satisfying my hunger
with nipples and clits
no need to be fancy
no need to be hip
just give me a diet of
nipples and clits
nipples and clits
nipples and clits
nothing as satisfying as
nipples and clits

POEMS FOR THE POET,
THE WORKING MAN,
AND THE DOWNTRODDEN
1999

FOR KEITH

his life was like
a bad luck gambler
dealt a losing hand
if he had 3 aces
the other guy
had a full house
forced to walk
the streets
like an undertaker
carrying a bag of bones

when he was down
no one was around
and when he was up
everyone else was down

women avoided him
like mustard gas
and poets testified
against him in mass
until he began
to resemble an eccentric
baseball pitcher
who couldn't remember
a win from a loss
forced to walk
the streets with
old treasure maps
looking for gold
and coming up craps.

COFFEE GALLERY BLUES

I don't care
how God Damn smart
they think they are
I'm bored with
their writing for themselves
just the other day
I heard one of them say
poetry isn't for the masses
it's been raining intellectual
snobs all day

POEM FOR A RADICAL FEMINIST

leaving the supermarket early
in the afternoon
I see this woman walking my way
with breasts the size of watermelons

she sees me staring
eying me suspiciously
when I make the mistake
of saying, "good morning"
and says, "FUCK YOU"
in a voice God himself
would be proud of

my eyes glance down
and see the button
she is wearing on
her sweater:
BALL BUSTERS.

I tip my hat and watch
her disappear into her VW
speeding away down
the street
leaving me to choke
on exhaust fumes

Main ain't nothing but
an ingrate
10 will get you
20 that it's a female
angel up there guarding
those pearly white gates

GRAND SLAM NIGHT

the lights are hot
the sweat beads bathe
his face like a lizard's tongue
the crowd is on its feet
screaming dancing whistling
stomping their feet
to the piped in music
of a marching band
he's making love to the mike
his words are thunder
lightning bolts appear from
the cracks in the ceiling
the book pages are burning
in his hands
the crowd is begging for more
he's running down the aisle
reciting the Ten Commandments
backwards
he's back on stage
doing acrobats
the audience is spellbound
the judges are writing down
their scores
he's standing on his head
he's trying to raise the dead
he's brought in the pope
they're doing a duet
the guy waiting his turn
looks white as a ghost

13 JAZZ POEMS
2000

OUTSIDE A BOARDED DOWN JAZZ CLUB

An old man stands in
The doorway
Of an abandoned building
Shoulders stooped
Jesus beard
Ragged clothes
Hands outstretched
Begging for his supper
A tote of wine

His prayers unanswered
Spittle on his chin
Holes in his shoes
Walt Whitman's forgotten
Child

PURE JAZZ

intense convoluted horn solo
old Diz filling the room
with his raging truth
Miles Davis and his lyric
savagery cutting to the bone
slicing its way to the center
force of gravity
lubricating the gears
of my mind
whose pigments of indigo
disguised as blue float
through the blue haze air
echoing latitudes of motionless
motion

DUKE ELLINGTON

December 1961
Duke Ellington concert
Sophisticated Lady - Mood Indigo
And "A Train"
Painting everyone with
Picasso blue
Riding each sound
To the end of the line
Lightning notes shimmering
Up and down my spine
Like a blind man
Tapping into raw emotion

JAZZ ANGEL

She sits alone
In her small hotel room
Above the 222 Club
8 months pregnant
Forced to give head
For soup and bread
No heat
One washcloth
One yellow stained washbasin
Hope bled dry
Immigrant without visa
Or status
An illegal caught
In a legal trap
Feels the baby stir
Move inside her
Lead Belly blues plays
Downstairs in the tavern
She heads for the door
Hears the night manager
Whisper, "Whore"
Suspended in silence
And grief
Floating face down
In the bowels
Of the American
Dream.

GHOSTS IN THE NIGHT

the shrill cry of dead
jazz greats ring out
in the night gliding
on dark rain clouds

jazz notes loud as thunder
burst the eardrums
like artillery fire
the 4-walls closing in
like a police dragnet

jazz luminaries beautiful
butterflies spreading
their wings
reshaping the stars
the universe
cosmic matter waiting
to be reborn

NORTH BEACH REVISITED
2000

FOR JAMIE

Sitting alone at the
Lost and Found Bar
Here in North Beach
Dark skin centuries
Removed from the present
Tapping your fingers to the
Late afternoon music coming
From the jukebox
No longer able to play
Your saxophone now
Sitting alone like you
Forgotten in a
Downtown pawnshop
Tagged for a quick sale

Someone puts a dollar
Into the jukebox and
Billie Holiday sings
Softly in your ear
Bringing an instant smile
To your face

A lighthouse beam
Dividing the thin line
Between sanity and madness
This is your turf
Your veins burning with
The energy of life
Long lines of images haunting
The afternoon hours

Bronzed warrior of old
Sitting here at the
Lost and Found bar
The beat forever going
On

FOR WILLIAM BURROUGHS

you played the game out
like a mafia don
late for an appointment with
the Godfather
living life with the tenacity
of a gunslinger
looking for another notch
on his gun
your cinematic midnight
cowboy eyes
cut-up poster boy
hero images walking
the mind's third eye
like a cyclops
trudging his way through
drug-induced mythologies
grinding away the days
the months the years
like a frenzied lap dancer
seeking thrills in forbidden
pleasure zones

NORTH BEACH DRUNK

I weave in and out of North Beach Bars
Ghosts at every bar stool
Drunk with memories of the past
Time capsule glimpses of fallen comrades
Flashing through my head
Lenny Bruce at the Purple Onion
William Margolis jumping out
A third story window
Looking for death and finding
Only paralysis
Echoes of the damned
Ring through my eardrums
Like cash registers
Playing a lonely concerto
Inside my head

CITY BLUES
2001

MADE IN THE U.S.A.

He toils on the assembly line
works an 8-10 hour shift
leaves a piece of him behind
for every part he helps make
at night, at home
he hides his thoughts
like smuggled contraband
sewn inside the false compartment
of a suitcase

He wears jeans made in Honduras
shoes made in Mexico
a shirt from Korea
a hat from Greece
makes love to his wife brought
over from Russia
with ruble eyes
and milky white thighs
that masks the capitalistic
lies

PANAMA MEMORIES 11

She lay there on the bed
Naked legs spread open
Labia lobster red
Her eyes those of a prisoner
Serving a life sentence
We never said a word
It was like a mechanic working
On a used car
Trying to put life back into it
Failing to get a response
Her eyes two headlights
Burned into the ceiling
As if she were taking inventory
Of all those there before me
A never-ending line
Of raw sausages moving down
An assembly line
In a butcher factory

OLD WOMAN

put away in an institutional
home
she watches television
all day
writes her daughter
tells her to come
and take her to the bank
so she can withdraw her money
and escape like the free bird
she once was

the daughter feels guilty
but knows she can't take
care of herself
and has her own life
to live

at night
the old woman ignores
the dinner bell
trapped in Dante's hell
where even enemies become
welcome visitors

I KISS THE FEET OF ANGELS
2001

I KISS THE FEET OF ANGELS

dark starry night
fog creeping in
over the hills
raindrops falling
on the window
I see the faces of old friends
staring at me
ghosts from the past
freight trains steam ships
subway trains carrying their
cargo of death
Rimbaud the mad hatter
Baudelaire
Lorca fed a dinner of bullets
Kaufman black messiah
walking Bourbon Street
eating a golden sardine
Micheline drinking with Kerouac
at the old Cedar Tavern
Jesus wiping the perspiration
from his forehead

the foghorn plays a symphony
inside my head
I hear the drums
I feel the beat
I kiss the feet
of angels

STATE OF AFFAIRS

academic verse
empty hearse
east coast
milk toast
west coast
holy ghost
ivy league
masturbation
forced elation
language school
end run
safe sex condom

WILL THE REAL
LAWRENCE FERLINGHETTI
PLEASE STAND UP
2002

Hey Lawrence
is it true that you said
when asked what you thought
of Jack Spicer,
"Isn't he the guy who drank
at Gino and Carlo's Bar?"

I mean I know you preferred
Mike's Pool Hall
back in the 50s
a much more polite atmosphere
and they made good sandwiches there.

Is it true what Eileen Kaufman says
that you ripped off royalties due
Bob Kaufman
who was too shell shocked
to know the difference?

Is it true what Plymell said
that you sold out his book
and sold the foreign rights to a German publisher
without Plymell seeing a dime?

And Bukowski told me in a letter
that you took 50% of foreign rights
when the standard contract calls
for 25%
He said he had to go to Nancy Peters
to get the amount owed him.

And did you call Richard Brautigan
a "lightweight?"
I remember reading that somewhere.

and did you call the longshoreman
Eric Hoffer the
Rod McKuen of philosophy?

And didn't you fail to show up
at the Folsom Prison Writer's Workshop
saying you had never been invited
and laughing to a group of admirers
gathered at the Café Trieste
that "it must have been a figment
of their imagination," not knowing
I had seen the letter myself.

And is it true that when Neeli
brought a group of students
to City Lights and explained the
history of the store to them
and read them a poem
that you got on the phone
and asked Neeli what the
hell he was doing reading poetry
that you were trying to run
a "damn business."

I don't know
maybe I'm dense
but it's hard for me to understand
how you can call yourself a revolutionist
when you've milked the system
like a dairy farmer
owning a prime piece of real estate
in the heart of North Beach
a home in Virginia
and a cabin in Big Sur.

I mean all that is good and well
but please don't compare yourself
with the likes of Lorca whose only
property owned was six feet of dirt
and congratulations on City Lights
being declared a landmark
I saw your party celebration list
not a single blue-collar poet listed
on the reading list.

I missed you at Micheline's memorial
and at Corso's too
I guess you had better things to do
but then didn't you dump your old pal
Shig after he had a stroke?
and came back to work for you
at City Lights only to find
his position had been filled.

Well no matter
you're a master of the PR game
you have the media in your back pocket
the literary crowd at your feet
but maybe you should think about
sending the San Francisco Police
a Christmas card each year
perhaps stuff in a few bucks
for good will
for without their busting you
for publishing HOWL
you would be just another
businessman scratching out
a living.

TRYING TO FIND
A COMMON BOND
2002

TRYING TO FIND A COMMON BOND

this young kid visited me
last year
from a small town in
the South or
the Midwest
I'm really not sure
I was half stoned
and don't care for visitors
these days
and I bought him a drink
and managed to bum him
a joint
and we talked about
the old days
when North Beach was alive
with creativity
but he wasn't totally satisfied
he wanted a woman
he wanted me to get him one
as if I were a pimp
and worse yet
I was forced to tell him
I can't even get one for myself
but he wouldn't believe it
he had read my poems
he had seen my book
Venus In Pisces
and maybe because
I had been a friend
of Bukowski
he felt that some
of the magic must have

rubbed off on me

when he went to play
the jukebox
I excused myself
to go to the bathroom
and while standing there
with my dick in my hand
I contemplated telling him
that we all lose it some day
some how somewhere
and that it would happen
to him too
sooner or later
if he insisted on believing
in fairy tales
and when I was through
relieving myself
I stepped out into
the back alley
and breathed in
the fresh air
and there was this dog
at the back
of another dog
humping away with
his tongue hanging out
and the other dog
looked bored
more or less
much like me
and I went back into
the bar
and against my better

judgment
put two dimes into
the public telephone
and dialed the number
of an older woman
I knew
who liked to fuck
young guys
but all I got
was a busy signal
and I knew as I headed
back to the table that
the kid would return
home
and write a poem about
how I had failed him
and I would go home
alone
and writer another poem
about how life
had failed me
in this we shared
something in common

REMEMBERING MY GRANDMOTHER

Oh how I hated that third street hotel
My grandmother old and wrinkled
Sitting in the main lobby with withered
Men and women reclining on worn couches
Staring off into space with eyes like
Death warrants
The smell of death
The smell of funeral parlors filling the stale air
My grandmother pale and sickly
Her voice trembling like an earthquake tremor
Rising to hug me
Wearing her years like rosary beads

Oh how I hated those visits
Watching those old people
Walk in and out of the hotel
On their way to a Sunday walk
Or a meal at a Tenderloin cafeteria
Looking like wasted corpses
On a 24-hour pass from the morgue
Living behind closed shades
In single light bulb rooms sealed
Like tombs
Walking in circles
Like a mad conductor
At an abandoned railroad yard

Oh how I hated those
Visits with death
Seeing my own mortality
In my grandmother's eyes

The old hotels are gone now
Torn down in the name of progress
But they will always exist
In the back of my mind
My grandmother walking the
Corridors of my skull
Reaching out to me with
Bone cold hands

These transitory images
That won't leave me alone
Fading in and out
Like a bad movie

Worn down, depressed
I struggle in the morning
To get out of bed
Cursed with an arthritic neck
Waking two, three times a night
With a full bladder
Trudging down the three flights
Of stairs to retrieve the
Morning newspaper

In and out of doctor offices
Taking pills like candy
Seeing my grandmother
In the dark gloom of that third
Street hotel
Death crouched low
Like a sprinter waiting the
Starter's gun

THE HOLY GRAIL
2002

FOR ALL THE KIDS WHO COULDN'T
GET ENOUGH OF BUKOWSKI

These kids could never
Get enough of him
Not in books or magazines
Or on rare occasions in person
They wrote poems for and
About him
They bemoaned the fact that
He hadn't been accepted
By the Academics
As if this were somehow
A liability
They flailed away
At the establishment
Supposedly on his behalf
But I suspect that getting
Their names in print
Had more than a little
To do with it

A few chastised him
For not using semicolons
But were quick to forgive him
Because he was a genius
And a genius can do
Whatever he wants to do

To his credit
When fame discovered him
He quit writing hate poems
To those who had once
Befriended him

And if success did this
To him
Then she can't be half
The whore they make her out
To be

For a man who lived alone
For most of his life
He did remarkably well
And if he conned the small
Press editors and publishers
It was only because
He had the stamps to do it
And selling your soul
To the post office
All those years
Was no easy trip
Believe me I know
I've been there
And the readings never
Came easy for him
Puking his guts out
Behind stage
Or in some bar bathroom
Or on that one occasion
In San Francisco
On the side
Of Ferlinghetti's van
But fate was kind to him
It gave him Linda Lee and
A new lease on life and
A home in San Pedro and
How many years
She tacked on to his life

We'll never know

He would be the first
To tell you that
He was an asshole and
He was
And so are you and I
Sometimes more and
Sometimes less
Depending on
The circumstances

He would be the first
To admit that
He was a hustler and
A con man and
He was both
But he did it with style
Which is more
Than you can say
For most of us

What he wouldn't tell
All those young kids
Was what they wanted
To hear the most
That yes they were
Poets
That yes their work
Was dynamite

That they too could
Make it
If only they

Hung in there
And flooded the littles
With their work
For the next
10 or 20 years
And the fates
Were kind to them
Failing that
There is always suicide
Or getting a job
At the
Post Office

Amen
Rest in peace.

A BASTARD CHILD
WITH NO PLACE TO GO
2002

DINING OUT WHEN I WAS YOUNG

I didn't like it when
My father took me with him
For lunch at Compton's Cafeteria
On Market and Van Ness
In San Francisco
It wasn't the food, which was
OK
But the old folks
The cook was fat and bald
And there was no waitress
The bus boy was old
And not a boy at all
And the people who came there
To eat
Were retired people
On low incomes
With death warrants for eyes
Dabbing at their turkey chins
With crumpled paper napkins
Looking like pallbearers
Back from a funeral

COCAINE ANNIE

Cocaine Annie biker queen
making love to the jukebox machine
hands caress well-curved hips
eyeing cowboy at the bar
digging her boots into the floor
wondering if he's worth a ride
tugging at her black leather jacket
slides hands down jean clad legs
heads out the door
opting for her Harley
gunning the engine
heading down 101
all the man she needs
vibrating between her well
shaped legs

WALKING THE STREETS LIKE A COWBOY
SEARCHING FOR A MIRACLE

I'm out walking the streets again
Like a crime scene photographer
Past Saint Paul's Church where
The smell of altar boys permeates
The air
The ripped up street still hot
From the smell of freshly laid tar

The tongues of harlots call out
Like hungry birds diving
For scraps of food
Passing over the head
Of the elderly priest
Standing on the church steps
Waving his hand in the air
As if carrying on
A private conversation with God
Extending his hand to a wrinkled
Italian woman talking into
Her rosary beads
Dusting off another miracle
Like an ageing cowboy
Looking forward to a night
On the town

TO BE A POET IN AMERICA

to be a poet in America
is to be faceless
like the Indian on
an old Buffalo head nickel
to be a poet
a prophet, a shaman
is Boxcar Willie riding
the rails without a guitar
to be a poet in America
is to be invisible

WHISPERS FROM HELL
2002

WHERE HAVE ALL THE POLITICAL POETS GONE

the old political poets don't read much anymore
content to scan the pages of major
literary journals, looking for their
names in print, their books reviewed
the old poets borrow lines from
their contemporaries, but only
when suffering writers block
the old poets no longer have
mother Russia to comfort them
the old poets have no parties to join
no Red Guard to march with
no parade to goose step too
the old poets sprinkle wheat germ
on their cereal and drink only
bottled water
the old poets forsake salt with
meals and take pride in the
little known fact that an average
spill of semen contains less than
twenty-five calories
the old poets have no causes
left to die for
no motherland to call their own
the old poets have turned in
their bombs and union cards
for chump change and social security
the old poets are tired
like Atlas they have learned the hard way
you can't carry the world on your shoulders
the old poets see life through
Dante's eyes
no longer able to distinguish

truth from lies
the old poets traded in
their party cards for government grants
and a shot at making GAP commercials
the old poets have sold out their dreams
realizing that suffering is overrated
the old poets have quit writing political poems
no longer carry Nietzsche inside
their head
the old poets ride the
poetry circuit pony express
grabbing for the gold ring
all too willing to sell themselves
for a lottery chance at fame

BACK THEN

Intelligence never got much further
than downtown Saigon
or a short trip to Da Nang
most of us were in the States
far behind enemy lines
doing our best to make the
world safe from the commie hordes

I remember one time
I interviewed a young marine
a victim of the "Tet" offensive
he talked about throwing
Cong out of helicopters
after interrogations
claimed the nightmares
left him sleepless
kept seeing all those faces
in, on between the walls
said a buddy of his
had sent home drugs concealed
inside body bags
but no one at the time believed him
tiny pieces of flesh hitting
him in the face
blood between what was left
of his chewed off fingernails
and fragging a Lieutenant
kept haunting him

Intelligence said that
he couldn't be trusted
he was either a basket case

or perhaps just wanted out
of the military
so they gave him
a three-day pass
just to play it safe
and set him up with
a V.A. shrink
not surprised when
he didn't show up

a week later
they found his body
down by the Beach Chalet
behind a forgotten old
WW 11 bunker

the bullet lodged
in his head
no bigger than the
guilt he left behind

TAKING THINGS IN
MY OWN HANDS
2003

MEMORIES

No more jazz at the
Black Hawk
No more jazz at the
Cellar
No more jazz in the
Fillmore
Just ghostly boarded down doors

Gone the clinking of glasses
The waitress who always knew
When your glass was empty
Working her magic on
Your inflamed nerve ends
The black female crooner
Hitting her notes
Like a midnight train
Breaking the stillness of night
With its long wailing whistle
Her sultry smile embedded
In your skin
Long after the closing hour
Leaving you sweating
Like waking from
A wet dream

POEM FOR ALL THE YOUNG TURKS

The more you commit yourself
The more they want
To dine on your flesh
These young Turks
From middle class America
Spoiled by affluence
Spoiled by the good life
Burned out before they turn forty
Taking potshots at you
In and out of print
Their lives strung-out
Like a series of bad dreams
Running through
The heads of defrocked priests
Hate crowded into their minds
Like a handful of sardines
In a fat man's mouth
Too safe to be anarchists
They talk of revolution
Looking toward tomorrow
But locked into yesterday
How they rant
How they rave
How they preach their
Holy Mantra
Hiding behind thin faces
And shaggy revolutionary
Beards
They make love
With butcher knife precision
And when the blood rushes
From the wounds

They pretend the shit
They smell is not their own

SLEEPING WITH DEMONS
2003

WORDS

each year the
words come harder
set their own pace
like a miler
sometimes the sprinter
sometimes the hare
always stripped bare

Bukowski told me
in a letter:
"You seem like a man
who knows where it's at."
    didn't then
        don't now.
just hanging around
waiting on the demon words
with images that dangle
like an outlaw's neck
stretched at the end
of a rope.

MIDNIGHT THOUGHTS

if there is a God
I mean, if there really
is a God, he must have stepped
out with my father for a smoke
the day I was born

just like him
just like God
to do some thing like that
on the most important day
of my life

I mean what do you expect
from someone who took a nap
the day his son was left
to hang out on that cross

but you really can't blame him
God I mean
miracles have a way of tiring
you out

EARLY MORNING INSOMNIA

sitting here alone with
a perpetual hard-on
4 in the morning
insomnia tearing at my guts
can't sleep, can't write
pussy on my mind
and people keep writing
and telling me I'm a legend
so why am I sitting here alone
staring into the dark
like a sniper fingering
a hair trigger
restless, unheroic
waiting on words that
won't come

THE SYSTEM
2003

FOLSOM PRISON

at Folsom Prison
the guards joke and laugh
as they have me empty my pockets
inside out
taking everything from me
leaving me with only my notebook
and a handful of poems
the guard in the watchtower
eyeing the prisoners
in the courtyard below
his hi-powered rifle
at the ready

the warden distrustful
perhaps even fearful
stations a guard outside
the small room where the
poetry workshop is held

the sharing of words
barely begins when
I look outside the window
see a bird on top of the
prison wall
free to come and go
as I turn my attention
to the guard in the back
of the room
hiding behind dark shades
looking more the outlaw
than the law

SAN QUENTIN PRISON

the tower guard surveys
the courtyard
gun at the ready
here in the museum
of the living dead

night shadows gather
dark as a tattoo
prisoners arriving
steady as labor pains
brought to their knees
by men with steel-tip boots
black as tar
with eyes that search
the cellblock
like a hungry wolf
in search of fresh meat

THE SYSTEM

There are old men and women
Who have worked all their lives
Who have put in thirty-five
And forty years for the right
To a pension

There are old people who have
Worked twenty years
Only to be laid off
Without so much as two weeks
Written notice
Abandoned to seek a living
At half the pay

There are old people
Who have worked
Most of their lives
Only to witness
The company go belly-up
And find there is no pension
Fund left

You can find them
On park benches
Or wandering lonely supermarkets
Or sitting daily
At neighborhood bars
Nursing their drinks
Like a blood transfusion

They come in different flavors
Like lifesavers

Some thin and balding
Some fat and sweating
Some complaining bitterly
Some too proud to let the
Pain show

So proud that they eat dog food
And find desert in back alley
Garbage cans
Trapped by false promises
Trapped by a belief in a system
That has abandoned them

For the most part
They suffer in silence and die unnoticed
To be carted off in a meat wagon
To be cut open by a coroner
Who sees them as morning cereal
Going about his business
As a butcher
Thinking of dinner
Thinking of a glass of wine
Thinking of getting laid
Thinking how it used to be
How it might have been
How it should have been

It's the way of life
It's the way of cockroaches
And mice

It's the system where
Just staying alive becomes
A small victory

THE OLD ITALIANS OF AQUATIC PARK

the old men of Aquatic Park
are dying or dead
they spend their time playing
bocce ball
lady death striking them down
like bowling pins
the old men of Aquatic Park
are steeped in tradition
dark skinned
dressed in sport shirts and slacks
looking like bit actors in a 1950s movie
dancing the last waltz
on the deck of the Titanic
the old men of Aquatic Park
sit on hard benches
late in the afternoon
their eyes moving left, right
front, center
as if at a tennis match
pausing to feed the pigeons
using their hands like cutting knives
to separate the crust from the bread
which they toss into the air
like rice at an Italian wedding
rising to brush the crumbs
from their baggy trousers
one with a suit vest and tie
pulling at the gold chain holding
his pocket watch
tucked securely next to his heart
the old men of Aquatic Park
have the smell of garlic and pasta

embedded in their skin
Italy beating in their hearts
the old men of Aquatic Park
are dying off with grace and dignity
and a love for the old ways

there is something sad
about being Americanized
there is something sad about
growing old
the bocce ball rolls slowly
along the grass
coming to rest like a hearse
parked next to an open grave
funerals wait on them
flowers scattered
like empty promises
the mourners growing fewer
in number
their ranks depleted
file slowly into their cars
disappear into the shadows
of late afternoon monotony

bocce ball will resume
in the morning
there are pigeons to be fed
wine to drink
stories to tell
the thirst for life masked
in the face of death

A.D. WINANS:
GREATEST HITS 1995-2003
2003

POEM FOR THE WORKING MAN AND THE YUPPIE

Some people guard their lives
Like a eunuch guards the
Harem door
Like a stock broker with
A hot tip
Like a banker who knows
That the dollar will only
Be worth half of what it is today
In less time than it takes to die
Better to linger over
A cup of coffee
Like a skilled lover with
No need for bragging rights
Remember that every newsman
On every corner in America
That every meat packer and fisherman
Knows more about life than
Your average poet
The blind man rattling
An empty tin cup
Makes more noise than
A yuppie gunning his
BMW
On his way to the
Graveyard

INSOMNIA

Tossing
turning
praying for sleep
when all else fails me
but God has no time
for insomniacs
and Christ must be busy
practicing for the resurrection

Falling asleep for an hour or two
head churning buttermilk dreams
the Holy Ghost stopping by for a chat
seems like an amicable chap
swapping stories from the past
just as if he were one of the boys
as I gradually surrender to his will
dreams lined-up like shots of tequila
at a Mexican brothel
only to wake again and again
insomnia a heavily armored
Spanish conquistador
takes no prisoners
plays your mind like a card shark
your body like a whore
in the morning
leaves you feeling
like bits and pieces of a shipwreck
washed up along the shore

WINTER POEM

It's been in the thirties two nights
in a row and my heater went out
and I'm sitting here freezing
my butt off with a hacking cough
waiting for the power company
to come and fix the problem
but it isn't so bad
when you consider 9/11
the war on Iraq
and that d.a. levy
took a rifle between his legs
and blew his brains out
which has nothing and yet everything
to do with this poem

Thirty-degree nights won't kill you
but they don't bring comfort either
the trouble with being single
the trouble with being 67
is knowing you could die alone
and go undiscovered for weeks
with nothing but rotting flesh
to tell your story
and a few poems to remember
you by

WHITMAN'S LOST CHILDREN
2004

OLD JOE

He sleeps in doorways
Or on park benches
Doesn't want to go
To a shelter
Not even when prodded
With the heavy weight of the
Beat cop's nightstick

Under threat of jail
He curls up
In a fetal position
And closes his eyes
Trying to shut out memories
Of Vietnam
Nightmares that whirl inside
His head like helicopter blades

The alcohol the drugs
The failed years gather
Like locusts inside the
Cranial guitar of his mind
Playing all night rhapsodies
Inside his head

Warrior troubadour
Of Pharaoh origins
Pale spokesman of lost tribes
Masked as a homeless transient

Poet, prophet
Of beauty and all
Its imperfections

Ravished by the streets
Kissed by angels
Left tired withered
Like an unattended
Kansas grain field

PARK POEM

in the park
a dog on a leash
denied his freedom
his master barking commands
the dog sits
pants, wags his tail
dreams a dog's dream
a fire hydrant
a buried bone
Snoopy defeating the
Red Baron
over the skies of Paris

the old man sits down
on the park bench
daydreams a young woman
and Adonis days
a man/a dog licking
their wounds

DREAMS THAT WON'T
LEAVE ME ALONE
2004

STYLE

I keep hearing this word over
and over again and again
endless talk about dressing in style
carrying yourself in style
as if it were a commodity
you might find at a convenience store
Babe Ruth had style
Clark Gable had style
Greta Garbo had style
Billie Holiday had style
Josephine Baker had style
Diamond Jim had style
Pontius Pilot lacked it
Lawrence Ferlinghetti
never had it
99 out of 100 poets lack style
but then poetry
has never been in style
style can't be learned
or bought
or bargained for
style can be lacking
in the richest of the rich
and stand out in a whore
style is a concept
style is the way people see you
style has never adequately
been defined in any dictionary
known to man
and never will

SITTING BULL

Sitting Bull
Poet of earth and water
You fought the white man's
Army to a stand still
Only to find yourself
Buffalo Bills sidekick
Sentenced to kill Custer
Over and over
To the cheers of wild West crowds
From horses and buffalo
To black exhaust fumes
Blue coated cavalry in every mirror
Forever branded with the
White mans scars

POEMS FOR THE CATHOLIC WOMEN IN MY LIFE

DEVOUT CATHOLIC

doesn't go all the way
but willing to lend
a helping hand

FALLEN CATHOLIC

in, out
knows what
it's all about

COMMERCIAL CATHOLIC

accepts tips
doesn't make
change.

A THING OF BEAUTY

it was at the Hotel Entella
before it burned down
her pubes dark as ash
set apart
from sheet white thighs
her scent an orchid
pinned to a virgin's chest

IN MEMORIAM
2004

FOR BOB KAUFMAN

You wore your life like a life preserver
Remembering forever the political chaos
Vietnam, George Jackson, King and the
Kennedy brothers
Tongue on fire
Mind carrying the music of Charlie Parker
And Mingus too
You walked the streets with
Edison electricity eyes
Vistim of shock treatments
And lies
With matted hair and soiled jeans
Disguising your nightmare dreams

You fired away with satellite precision
And the Gods feared your thunder
Your eyes boring through the
Living dead
Walking unmasked for all to see
While death a circus clown
Followed you about town
Oblivious to the gothic nightmares
You wore like an anchor around
Your neck

You moved through the streets
Of North Beach
The original be-bop man
Poet in residence caretaker
Of the clan
The haunting breath of death
Snapping at your footsteps

Like a hound dog closing in
For the kill
And when the magic
Of North Beach left
You did too
Moving to the Bayview
Black ghetto away from the
Social zoo
A living Bangladesh come true
Your words to the end
Hard as a pair
Of new boots
Echoing across the universe
Like King Tut's curse
And when death came
To claim you
The angry ghosts of the
Co-existence Bagel Shop
Beat hard in the paper hearts
Of every city cop
The shadow of your being
Dancing from Chinatown alleys
To downtown high rises
Billie Holiday forever singing
In your heart

FOR WILLIAM WANTLING

Looking into the cracked lips of sorrow
I walk the harsh streets of tomorrow
The ghost of my fears demanding that
I face my destiny
But I am not a graveyard poet
In search of chilled bones
The words I speak hold no fear
For like you
I have tasted the laughter of life
Walked the sinister circus of reality
Playing out the game like
A chess master
Knowing there is no power
Strong enough to still
The song inside you

The long years of silence
The grave brings can only
Be broken by those who care enough
To take up the cause
There are those who seek
The underground warmth
Desire to be closeted in blackness
Moths of night with closed minds
And hardened hearts encased in stone
And then there are those like you
Who sense to be a poet
One must first die

Inspiration comes naturally
Expiration takes effort
It is not enough to passively die
You must expel life while living

This is the mark of the true poet

The night rolls back its wings
Teeth as cold as naked bone
But neither the night nor
The poet dies quietly
Only the flesh expires
The words linger on welcoming
The taste of ash
And morning comes as no loss
For wherever you are
You survived the pain
Refused to surrender
Earth's flesh removed from reality
Here in the wakening of dawn
Where the mist smells sweetly
And one can hear the throats
Of birds singing like cannons
In the hour when the spirit
Collects its visions
Replaying them on old walls
Gatsby shots from another era
Stills to fill the void
In a world of runaway tongues

You are everywhere beneath
The wild grass
The silver star of night
The face of morning
The crystal clear sky singing
Your song
Gone with others
Who dared to hold
The sun in their hands

THE WRONG SIDE OF TOWN
2005

THE WRONG SIDE OF TOWN

cop's flashlight intruding
on my thoughts
loud rapping on car window
demanding to know what I'm doing
out on the other side of town
at this ungodly hour

ordered out of car
frisked and taken downtown
for questioning
police suspicious
why would a white boy
be listening to a tape
by a black musician
in a respectable part
of town

SATURDAY NIGHT HAPPENINGS

The air has that stale cigarette smell
Rancid as spoiled meat
The men in blue work the crime scene
Laying down yellow tape and chalk lines
That circle the corpse riddled with bullets
Swiss cheese street justice

The people pushed back behind the barrier
Mill around like autograph seekers
Waiting on a Hollywood matinee idol
Go home the mustached cop says
Bullhorn in hand, go home
No story here, go home
One more drive-by shooting
One more Saturday night death
Waiting on a Sunday morning headline
Go home
no story here
Go home
no story here

68

lines beginning to form
at the corner
of my eyes
and I eat not from hunger
but out of force of habit
the fire in my loins is still there
and the hose still hard
just no one to man it

THIS LAND IS NOT MY LAND
2006

PANAMA ONE

In Panama City
The day they killed
The President
A group of us were given rifles
And a loaded clip
And told to assist
The Panama National Guard
In whatever way we could
Like rousting civilians
Who might be possible assassins

We split off from
The rest of them
Six of us
Four half-drunk
And one stoned on grass
And dumb me wanting
To be anywhere
But there
When we came across this woman
Working in the fields

And what started off as questioning
Turned out to be a strip-search
Eager hands violating
Every part of her body
And when I protested
I was told to shut up
Or get with it

They laughed that
They were just looking

For concealed weapons
Wrestling her to the ground
As I walked away in shame
Not wanting to be part of
What I had no chance
Of stopping

PANAMA TWO

1955 the
President of Panama
Gunned down at the race track
For building schools and roads
And thinking of the people

Elite unit troops issued guns
And sent to town
To roust civilians
In the streets

Two hours into forced insanity
I sneak off to the Amigo Bar
And smoke a joint in silence
Trying to shut out the madness
Until I am oblivious to what
Is happening outside
Half the men looking for
An assassin
The other half
Too stoned to care

The sweet smell of Mary Jane
Floats through the air
Filling the bar
As I put on the safety
And lay my rifle to one side
Smiling at the bar girl
On the other side of the bar
Not knowing whether
She would like to make
Love to me
Or put a bullet
In my head

PANAMA SIXTEEN

"What the hell were you thinking?"
the sergeant asked me
planting a hard one into
my gut
as I sucked air into my lungs
"We have a duty here
an obligation to our hosts"
he bellowed
as I nodded my head
and braced myself for another
blow
watching him pace back and forth
his face red with anger
"How in the hell do I explain this
to the old man (Colonel)"
He said more to himself than me
his anger exploding
into a string of curses
but all I could think of was
the sea of brown faces
brave enough to face the
National Guardsmen
and how they stared
them down
until the jeeps arrived
from over the hill
with mounted machineguns
firing over the heads
of the student protestors
and although I knew
I shouldn't be there
I stayed and was detained

with the rest of them
taken downtown to the
police station
and put in a holding cell
one backed-up toilet
for fifty or more of us
the stench of urine
and shit making me gag
fish heads and rice
for dinner
my white face standing out
like a bad prop
in a failed play
knowing I had failed
in my duty
not to bring dishonor
on our unit
so I played the game
by the rules their rules
and paid my penance
bowed to the sergeant
a religious man
who took me under
his wing
and had me baptized
into the Lutheran faith
but was never able
to cleanse the
window of my soul

THE WORLD'S LAST RODEO
2006

NEW YEARS DAY POEM

Come in
    Sit down
And I'll make you
    A cup of tea
We'll leave our insecurities
    At the door

Pull up a chair
Take off your shoes
The telephone ringer is off
The doorbell disconnected

No television with its war news
No stereo to startle the ears
No negative thoughts of the past
No regrets

I apologize for the lack
    Of a fireplace
        And the empty wine bottle
Perhaps a smile to warm the
    Heart will do

You are welcome here
This is a new year
A new day

Come in
    Sit down
Make yourself
    At home

RAIN POEM

The storm
Lets up

The birds
Take flight

Neighbor's dog
Shakes water

Drops in sprinkler
Like fashion

A cavalry
Of children

Magically appear
In rainbow splendor

Sun peaks
From clouds

Smell of spring
In the air

HAIKU

A microphone inside my head
Static playing mad tunes on my tongue
A lonely grasshopper without wings

HAIKU 11

Another day spent home alone
Bag lady talks to cracks in the sidewalk
Pope takes his last breath

HAIKU 111

Kaufman poems rattle inside head
Hunter Thompson gunshot wound bleeds the dawn
Umpire in black sweeps off home plate

SOUTH OF MARKET
2006

HOW TO SPOT A YUPPIE

they are young and have ambitious
looks about them
they wear expensive clothes
with gold jewelry adorning their necks
they hang out at trendy restaurants
parking their Lexus or BMW
in front of fire hydrants
as they show off their stock portfolios
while sipping white wine
looking like they just returned from
a trip to Mexico
casual yet serious looking enough
that not a strand of hair is out of place
you can find them on any given weekend
playing tennis or jogging near a mall
they look like they want something
and are willing to kill
to get it

LOOKING BACK

When I was twenty
It was a ball
There were no thoughts
About the right one
It was just this one
And that one booze music
And fun
When I was thirty the
Search began
It became a bit more than
Flesh and bone
And I began to think
Of marriage children
And a home
Tired of hangovers
Bent retching over a toilet bowl
The searching of the soul
When I was forty
Doubts began to set in
Memories of my mother breaking
A dish over my father's head
A lover long dead
Young women passing
In and out of my bed
When I was fifty the women
Began to walk it past my door
And the bars became a bore
But the search went on
Now at seventy
My spirit on the run
I no longer play the game
Having escaped the mad house

Having escaped the nursing home
Is a small victory in it self
The graveyards are filled with
Lovers who search for the right one
Only to rot under the
Weight of the sun

THE OTHER SIDE OF BROADWAY
2007

OLD WARRIOR OF NORTH BEACH

He walks the streets of North Beach
looking like an old man
with eyes empty as a broken parking meter
Unemployable weighed down by the years
His mind heavy as an anchor
dragging the ocean floor

Forgotten rebel playing old Lorca ballads
in the shipwreck of his heart
His mind destroyed by shock treatments
and one too many police batons

At night he dreams he is riding with Geronimo
Has imaginary conversations with Charlie Parker
Rides the ferry with Coltrane and Mingus
Getting off at Bourbon Street to down
A drink with Kerouac

He shares a cigarette with Charlie Chaplin
at the Bijou Theater
Walks the battlefields with Walt Whitman
Rides the plains with Red Cloud
in search of the last buffalo

Walking the streets of North Beach
in search of the elusive ginger fish smell
Death a sightless chauffeur waiting
Like a concubine facing another
Apocalyptic day

CITY POET

Once addiction sets in
There is no stopping it
You become a serial killer
Attacking the keyboard at will
Your mind works in shifts
Strange creatures live inside your head
Show no mercy give no ground
Forcing your fingers to do their bidding
Writing down their thoughts in your
Loose-leaf notebook

The city is your slaughterhouse
Like a wife it accommodates your moods
Doesn't seem to mind you giving
Her a bad name

You walk her streets a hungry vampire
Lapping up your own blood
On nights when blood transfusions
Are not enough

MARKING TIME
2008

LI PO ON MY MIND

spring flowers in bloom
nature's wild children

a sailing boat making its way
through San Francisco Bay

water calm
as whispering wind

a flock of seagulls plaintive call
auditioning for God's choir

two old men play chess
under the shade of a tree

I mark time
like Li Po
mixing words with
wine

RAIN DAY POEM

A hawk hovers over the field
A mouse sits still in the weeds
Ageless trees stretch toward the sky
A Hawk
    A mouse
        Giant ageless trees
A Choir in the cathedral of life

DAYS IN HEAVEN NIGHTS IN HELL
2009

UNITED AIRLINES CRASH IN IOWA JUNE 1, 1989

Here they come
To rest among the
Long rows of corn
Sprawled like litter
Some in pieces
Some with no pieces at all
Serenaded by the howling wind
Lying among scraps of metal
Like tiny pieces of loose thread
Falling from the eye of a needle
Life a never-ending series of tragedies
Stretching the skin like a bad tattoo
Motionless bodies lined-up like
Bowling balls
A sadness so great so large
That no closet can contain it
The rescuer workers searching the
Wreckage for signs of life
Matching limbs spread out
Across the yellow cornfields
Resembling old band leaders
Unconvinced the dead
Cannot dance

LETTING GO

The last desperate thread of love
A shoe print in the mud
Next to the public phone booth
Her talking to her new beau
Not noticing the love beads
I bought her in Mendocino
Left behind in the circle
Of my footprint
Like a tribal elder offering
A small piece of his heart

BILLIE HOLIDAY ME
AND THE BLUES
2009

FOR JACK MICHELINE

He was a high note
Of wailing jazz
The spark that ignites
A fire
He was a shot of heroin
A fifth of Jim Beam
A shaman a con man
A vagabond poet
Who shuffled words like
A riverboat gambler
Ravished by illness
Ravished by time
He painted his visions
On canvas
On city streets
In bars in coffee houses
His poems racing across the
Streets of America
Pure innocence
Pure genius
Poor jazz
Spinning words that
Hung in mid-air
Like a hummingbird
Drunk on the
Pollen of life

THE BLACK HAWK 1962

The old Black Hawk booked the
Best jazz musicians of its day
Getz, Miles Davis, Diz
Just to name a few

I went there but twice
Once with the poet
Jack Micheline
Once with a young
Latina girl
To see Miles Davis
Blow his magic
Forced to sit in the
Teen-age section
Because she was only
17
Sipping on a coke
High on the high note
Smoke curling around the room
In long lingering lazy circles
Sweet sax
Smooth gin fizz
My hand on warm thigh
Feeling high
Feeling cool
Be-bop rhythms dancing
Inside my soul

NO ROOM FOR BUDDHA
2009

POEM FOR MY MOTHER

My mother's eyes stare at me
Like a wounded doe
Looking into a rifle scope
The months grow antlers
The years fangs
Time a barbed wire fence
Tears at the soul
Her smile fading
Like watercolors off
A worn canvas
The shadow of my ancestors
Stalks my dreams
Like an aging warrior
Tracking game
My mother's eyes smoldering
Like hot ashes
In a Hiroshima graveyard

UN TITLED

I'm addicted to looking at pictures
My mother left behind
From assorted photo albums
Bringing back memories of our family
Flat on Page Street
Teddy the family dog chasing his tail
Like dad chased his dreams
Mother sitting on the sofa knitting
A heating pad on her swollen feet
Or working a crossroad puzzle
One eye on sister the other on me
Dad lighting up a cigarette
Blowing smoke rings across the room
It's like reliving vaudeville days
My father a grip-man on the
Old Muni Railway
Taking me with him for a ride
Letting me ring the bell
A look of pride in his eyes
When he said to the passengers,
"That's my son"
May be the only memory
I had of childhood fun
Father and son as one
Riding to the end of the line
That one time when everything
In life was fairytale fine
Now at sixty-five
I feel like a dinosaur
Walking the ends of earth
With nothing but scraps
To feast on

TWO POEMS FOR MY FATHER

1.

On weekends my father
Worked for Luke Morley
At the corner grocery store
Not for money but for conversations
He never had with my mother
Staying there until late at night
Stacking shelves with canned goods
Coming home with his reward
A pack of two of cigarettes
Sitting alone in the living room
Staring out the window
Blowing smoke rings in the air
The ashes falling in the ashtray
Like bits and pieces of his life

11.

I turn on the baseball game
On TV
And Barry Bonds is giving
A rare interview
And in the background
Players are shagging fly balls
And I'm back at Golden Gate Park
And my father is hitting fly balls
Which I'm to catch in my newly bought
First Baseman's glove
And I circle around reach up
And misjudge the flight of the ball
And it hits me flush in the nose
And I drop the glove and start crying
And my father yells at me
To put the glove back on
My mother trying to comfort me
As my sister, always the tomboy,
Runs out and picks up the glove
And tells my father to hit her one
Which she catches flawlessly
And I see the proud look
In my father's eyes
The penance I paid
All those years into adulthood
A heavy weight laid to rest beneath
Six feet of cold hard earth

LOVE — ZERO
2010

#6

the day after Christmas
I wear you like a pressed flower
recently unwrapped presents spread
out in the living room
the house still surprisingly warm
caught in a storm that needs no words
in a soft place inside the heart where
all language stops

#8

making love to you
is like owning a Picasso
you make me feel like
a drunk Jesus walking
on water
God Jesus and the
Holy Ghost rolled
into one

#20

twice we have broken up
and I tell you the next time
like baseball it's three strikes
and you're out
but you think I'm like a boomerang
always coming back
as I sit here alone in bed tonight
overcome with a great sadness
thinking of all the times
your body so close
and yet so far away
your eyes telling their own story
like an angry ghost reclining
in a three-legged rocking chair

AUDIENCE OF ONE

Old songs with half forgotten lyrics
play with my head
older still movies play on the
bark of my skin
Oklahoma, South Pacific, West Side Story
singing on the tip of my tongue
humming my way back to yesterday
left alone with ghostly echoes
serenading the dead

I can almost feel the ignited passion
lost lovers draped on my bed
tasting the melody riding up and down
my spine
memories of my parent's old victrola
vinyl records spinning
on a balanced groove
a love affair so fragile
it was like trying to thread a needle
in the teeth of a storm
fading
fading
fading now
like an old flame sipping
on a cup of coffee
at my favorite café
a smile on her face
fingers snapping feet tapping
to the music that made us as one

evaporating in the face of dawn
like clouds taking foreign shapes

like the smoke rings my father
blew my way as a child
Frank Sinatra crooning in the
background

the way of music
    sex
        love
            god
                and death
playing to an audience of one

BLACK LILY
2010

Black Lily wheels her whip
Leaving red marks on
White skin

Lily hums old plantation
Slave songs that
Her clients do not comprehend
Bent on knees worshiping
Her black skin
Her whip rising and falling
On their back

Lily Knows that
They will be back
Like a gambler addicted
To the race track

Lily all dressed
In black.

Lily traded in her broom and mop
For a cat-of-nine tails and
A riding crop

The sting of her whip bringing
Back memories of her grandmother's
Slave ship

Lily dressed in leather
Mistress supreme
Knows how to make
White boys scream

Black Lily has the man
Of the hour under
Her power
Knows that soon
She will have him crawling
Making pig like sounds
All senses heightened
From Nipples to bowels
Waiting eagerly for
Her intrusion
Like a ruptured patient
In need of a transfusion

DANCING WITH WORDS
2010

BAYSHORE JUNKYARD

What's left of a classic 1956 Chevy
Lies like a war zone corpse
In a deserted battleground
Hubcaps gone seats gutted
Steering wheel pushed
Into dashboard
Waiting on the auto crusher
To clutch her in its steel claws
To come down on her
Like a serial killer
Mutilated raped ravished
All life squeezed out of her once
Virgin frame

MEXICO 2008

Alone in my hotel room
In Mexico, thirty-six hours
Before my flight back
To San Francisco
A hundred blank pages
Rattling around inside my head

I can turn each one
Into paper airplanes
Fly them to imaginary places
Or write poems on them in vivid old
Mexico song rhythms

If I could draw
I'd draw a rainbow picture
Of beautiful Indian women
With faces brown as earth

Soon I'll return to San Francisco
City of dreamers drunkards
And lonely lovers
I will turn the blank pages
Into poems fleshed from the
Pond of my memory bank
Baited with the history of old
Mexico

www.ingramcontent.com/pod-product-compliance
Lightning Source LLC
Chambersburg PA
CBHW070016100426
42740CB00013B/2516